Founding Philosophers

Using the Wisdom of America's First Generation to Solve Today's Problems

For my amazing children, who have captured my heart in ways I never imagined. May they always live in a country where they are free to reach their potential and enjoy their God given rights. And for my beautiful wife who's support makes all things possible.

Contents

Introduction...5

Chapter 1: Why Should We Care?...................................8

Chapter 2: The Nature of Rights........................23

Chapter 3: The Founders and Religion...................36

Chapter 4: The Founding and Social Welfare............50

Chapter 5: America's Legacy of Property Rights.........61

Chapter 6: The Judiciary...............................72

Chapter 7: Foreign Policy..............................81

Chapter 8: The proper Role of Government..............93

Chapter 9: The Right way Forward......................100

Afterward..107

Introduction

America faces an uncertain future. Decades of over-reaching and unconstitutional government programs have left the greatest nation ever created mired in high taxes and social welfare. Trillions of dollars are being spent annually to redistribute wealth in the largest government sponsored theft in history. America's standing in the world is steadily eroding as these policies eat away at the national vigor of the populace and threaten to change America from a republic built on individual liberty and rugged self reliance into just another socialist country like those of Europe.

I believe all of these problems are the result of our straying, as a nation, from the basic philosophies of our Founding Fathers. Those brave and brilliant men addressed all of the problems we have today in their writings and rhetoric. We can solve any political or economic problem by examining the aggregate wisdom of their individual philosophies. That is why I wrote this book. It is my sincere hope that through education of the founding philosophy of America we can turn this ship around.

This book is fundamentally a philosophical discussion. It is written in the first person; a fact that I'm sure would make every one of my English teachers cringe in disgust, but I did that for a very good reason. Far too often philosophy is regarded as too boring or too ethereal for practical application because it is lost in the flowery language of the ancients or the sterile language of modern academics. I wanted to make our Founding Fathers' philosophy personal, because to them it was personal. Free trade was not the domain of ivory tower economists or just another theory coequal with socialism. It was often the difference between a thriving economy and rebellion. Freedom of speech was not a sophomoric excuse for flag burning and pornography. It was something every one of them witnessed friends and family die to protect. The right to bear arms was not a 'collective right' as so many on the left would have us believe. It was and remains a necessary extension of our God given right to defend our families and an important safeguard against the encroachment of government.

Another facet of this book that the reader will immediately notice as unique is the documentation. I chose to use footnotes in lieu of the standard bibliography. I did this because I want my research to be right in front of you so you can quickly see where my information came from and how I used it. It is important to look beyond the mere words of a book and see how the writer was informed if one is to understand its true context.

A republic cannot survive without a populace well educated in its history and founding philosophy. Please do not end your education with this short book. *Founding Philosophers* should be a beginning, not an end to your education. There is a wealth of knowledge and wisdom available if you simply choose to look for it. As you will see, much of my research was accomplished on the Internet. I made every effort to use .gov and .edu resources. The Internet can be a swamp of misinformation, but there is also a lot of gold out there too. Understanding how to properly use it can make researching the founding era much faster and easier.

In order to be a more responsible American voter you must read the writings of our Founders and their philosophical predecessors. Read the Federalist Papers, the correspondence of John Adams and Thomas Jefferson, James Madison's minutes of the Constitutional Convention and go another step further. Read the writings of people like John Locke, Adam Smith and Edmund Burke and read for yourself the same words that inspired the generation of 1776 to throw off the yoke of oppression and confront headlong what was at the time the most powerful empire in the history of mankind. Most of all, read, reread and read again the Constitution. Memorize the Bill of Rights, understand that it was not meant to be a 'living document', but an everlasting bedrock for our civilization and apply it literally to each and every vote you cast.

Chapter 1
Why Should We Care?

Never can tyranny be introduced into this country by arms; these can never get rid of a popular spirit of enquiry... It is to be subverted only by a pretence of adhering to all the forms of law and yet breaking down the substance of our liberties.[1]

Alexander Hamilton spoke these words while arguing before the New York Supreme Court on behalf of a man accused of libel in 1804, but I believe they ring truer today than ever before. In Hamilton's time most people feared tyranny in its most naked form. After the bloody and very nearly failed Revolutionary War, most assumed that if their hard won liberties were wrenched away it would be by a foreign king and his invading hordes or a violent uprising from within. At the very least, many assumed, an overreaching legislature or president whose actions would be obvious would destroy them.

Hamilton, however, understood a truth that has taken hundreds of years to reveal itself; Americans' God given liberties cannot be stolen at the point of a sword or the muzzle of a gun, if we are to lose this precious gift of liberty it will be by individuals who promise the world. It

---

[1] Brookhiser, Richard, *Alexander Hamilton: AMERICAN*, Simon and Schuster, 1999

will be taken piecemeal by government programs aimed at improving our lives... so long as we forfeit a little bit of money here and small portion of freedom there. Eventually each little compromise will add up until one day we all awake to an America were the Federal Government controls every aspect of our lives. Even things as mundane as light bulbs and table salt will flow through an army of bureaucrats before we use them. In short, we will have freely given away our liberty to secure the false promises of economic equality and social justice.

We see this today in the machinations of liberal politicians of both parties. I have no doubt that the architects of healthcare reform, cap and trade, illegal alien amnesty and the vast welfare state have deluded themselves into believing they are doing good for society. Unfortunately, the intended and unintended consequences of such government actions erode the foundations of liberty that have made America a shining city upon a hill and the last best hope of mankind.

Hamilton was not simply defending a client in the courtroom. He was warning posterity of the very real danger of soft tyranny. It goes by many names: the nanny state, statism, socialism, liberalism and even, surprisingly, compassionate conservatism. However, the result is always the same. In the long run these policies always destroy free markets and erode liberties. They cause class based and race based strife as corrupt politicians pit the haves against the have-nots in order to use the force of the ballot box to keep their jobs and enrich themselves.

We see all of this coming to fruition today. Our national debt is out of control and getting worse. The Federal Government has taken control of our healthcare industry, one of our economy's largest sectors. There is the real possibility that Washington will force artificial limits on industries' carbon emissions, effectively capping the size of our economy and trading away our children's future. Local and state governments are getting into the act by enacting nanny state laws such as those proposed in New York that would regulate table salt in restaurants and using the principle of eminent domain to steal private land from law abiding private citizens.

At the time of this book's writing the Republicans retook control of the House of Representatives, riding a wave of Tea Party support for smaller government. It is a step in the right direction, but remains to be seen if the Grand Old Party can abandon their spendthrift ways, stem the tide of socialism and get America back on track. The truth is no party can do it. Only the vigilance of the people can repel the insidious advance of socialist forces.

THE SIREN SONG OF SOFT TYRANNY

What is soft tyranny? Hard tyranny is obvious to all. It is the violent oppression of one group over another. It can be physical, economic or religious. NAZI Germany, Imperial Japan, Soviet Russia and Communist China with their wholesale slaughter of millions of innocent people, are obvious examples. The religious persecution of Jews and Christians in the Middle East and the former policies of apartheid in South Africa are also obvious examples of hard tyranny. Soft tyranny is much more insidious. That is not to say it is worse. We are not and most likely never will be any where close to such terror as Americans, even if we do surrender all our rights. It is insidious, though, because its promises of a better future for all lure people away, happily, from their natural state of liberty until they realize all too late they gave away their children's futures for concepts that cannot exist in the real world.

Would you make decisions that you knew would make life more difficult for your children? Would you encourage them to become less educated, take lower paying jobs and become more dependent on government for their daily sustenance? Would you finance extravagant vacations and luxury cars with debt that your children and grandchildren would be required to pay? Of course not! Such behavior would amount to unconscionable abuse on the part of the parent, but that is what we have done to our children and ourselves for nearly a century.

Each consecutive generation for almost 100 years has added more and more social welfare programs. Social Security, Medicare, Medicaid, The Great Society and health care reform are just the biggest of thousands of government programs. Each one promises miracles like extending healthcare to everyone, lowering costs or ensuring an easy retirement for all, but instead they push our country farther into debt, deteriorate the nuclear family and lure millions from the productive sector of society into becoming wards of the state.

The Founding Fathers realized this would happen if the federal government, or any government for that matter grew too large. This is why William Patterson, signer of the Constitution and our nation's first Attorney General worried that eventually democracy would lead to a country where people voted themselves their neighbors' money creating "a set of drones or of idle extravagant wretches [who] live upon the earnings of others".[2] James Madison shared this gloomy view. By the 1820's he was convinced the country would eventually reach a point where class struggle and people's lust for others' property would lead to "contests and antipathies not dissimilar to those between the Patricians and Plebeians of Rome".[3] What is the heart of our nation's social spending if it is not just that, people using the ballot box to legalize the theft of other people's money? All of our well-meaning social programs are really nothing but theft. And it makes no difference that it is poor people stealing from rich people.

[2] Flynn, Daniel. *Why the Left Hates America: Exposing the Lies that have Obscured Our Nation's Greatness.* Prima Publishing. 2002. P. 205
[3] West, Thomas G. Vindicating the Founders: Race, Sex, Class and Justice in the Origins of America. Rowman and Littlefield. 1997. P.127

Theft is theft and all Americans, rich and poor alike are worse off in the long run.

THE ECONOMIC CONSEQUENCES

We all recognize that there are certain things the federal government must spend money on. Only the federal government can support a military, an effective post office or a space program. We need the federal government to spend money to maintain roads, secure the border and regulate commerce. Furthermore, we expect the government to pay for these things with real money, not endless cycles of debt upon more debt and not by printing money until it is worthless.

It is no secret that our national debt is out of control and will soon bankrupt our nation if something is not done. However, too often we blame the constitutionally sanctioned institution of military spending as the major culprit. For years we have been inundated with headlines like this one from USA Today in 2005: *War Cost Drives Record Deficit*. The first paragraph of the article says:

The Bush administration said Tuesday it will need at least $80 billion more to pay for the wars in Iraq and Afghanistan and other foreign policy priorities, pushing the total military and reconstruction tab beyond $300 billion. The new spending would make this year's federal budget deficit the largest in history.[4]

It isn't until the end of the article that we learn the deficit was already $368 billion before figuring in the cost of the war. So $80 billion dollars is driving the record deficit, but the $368 billion mystery figure does not? How

---

[4] "War cost drives record deficit". USA Today Jan 25th 2005.
http://www.usatoday.com/news/washington/2005-01-25-budget-deficits_x.htm

can that be? Later in the article it is revealed that the cost of the wars in Iraq and Afghanistan combined amounts to $5.1 billion dollars a month. What is not said is that much of that money would still be spent by the military on training and upgrading equipment, even if the wars never happened.

What the progressives in the media and government do not want you to know is that socialism is the true driving force behind our record deficits, not the past decade's war. We can debate until the end of time whether the war in Iraq was a moral and strategic imperative or a colossal blunder, but it never occupied more than a tiny fraction of our national debt. There is plenty of fat to trim in our defense spending, but it pales in comparison to what we spend on the redistribution wealth.

According to the Congressional Budget Office the 2010 federal budget includes $687 billion for defense. However, the top three social programs combined account for nearly $1.5 *TRILLION*. They are $695 billion for Social Security, $516 billion for Medicare and $284 billion for Medicaid. Other expenditures include $21 billion for "community and regional development", $71.4 billion for "education, training, employment and social services" and $63 billion for "income security" otherwise known as unemployment and welfare.[5]

We see in government spending how we have lost our way as a nation. Our government considers Social Security, Medicare and Medicaid "mandatory spending" and defense "discretionary spending" even though the Constitution requires the federal government to spend money on defense while prohibiting spending on the others.

All of this unconstitutional spending adds up to enormous debt. According to Treasurydirect.gov the

---

[5] *Comparison of Projected Revenues, Outlays, and Deficits in CBO's March 2009 Baseline and CBO's Estimate of the President's Budget*, p.9-11
http://www.cbo.gov/ftpdocs/102xx/doc10296/TablesforWeb.pdf

national debt on the day I wrote this page (Jan 5, 2011) was $14,014,049,043,294.41.[6] This is money that must be paid back and the government only has three basic options. It can raise taxes, print more money or cut spending. The first two options take money directly out of our pockets and our children's pockets. The third option is a direct assault on the power of the Federal Government. Guess which ones Congress and the Executive always choose.

There are literally thousands of government programs. Their costs range from hundreds of thousands to hundreds of billions. We are told these programs will make life better for all of us or help those who have been victimized by our greedy ways, but in reality the opportunity cost of social justice far out weighs any supposed benefits.

Every dollar we spend on government programs, whether it is for a constitutionally mandated program like the military or an unconstitutional one like healthcare reform, is a dollar less we can spend building family businesses, or sending our children to college. Every dollar we pay in taxes is a dollar less we can spend renovating our homes or putting people to work building skyscrapers and airplanes. But the worst part of all is there are millions of real people in our country who have become so reliant on these programs that they have no other means of supporting themselves. They have become the "set of drones... [who] live upon the earnings of others" that William Patterson warned us about. As these people begin to occupy a larger portion of the nation's voting population, what is to stop them from permanently instituting the theft of everyone else's hard earned money?

People unable to support themselves and dependent on government for life's basic necessities; that is the true legacy of our social spending. Social Security,

---

[6] http://www.treasurydirect.gov/NP/BPDLogin?application=np

for example, was supposed to be a way for people to save for retirement and spend their golden years in much deserved leisure, living out old age with dignity. Instead it only encouraged generations of people to NOT save for retirement and expect the government to take care of them in old age. Now the younger generations are stuck paying the bill while millions of elderly can't even afford to feed themselves unless some government bureaucrat cuts them a check. Where is the dignity in that?

The Heritage Foundation, a Washington D.C. based think-tank and one of the greatest sources of real, constitutionally sound solutions to our nations problems has for some time now been publishing an index of government dependence. It measures the number of people that depend on government for some or all of their housing, retirement, health and welfare, education and agricultural services. They used the year 1980 as the base and gave that year a score of 100 for comparison purposes. The index's score for 1962 is 19. That means Americans were 1/5 as dependent on government in 1962 as they were in 1980. The score for 2009 is 272! That means that Americans are almost three times more dependent on government for their basic survival as they were when I was born and 14 times more dependent on government than my grandparents' generation was in 1962.[7]

These are sobering numbers. Quite frankly I believe our Founding Fathers would be utterly ashamed of us all. It would appear that our nation has ceased to be populated by the rugged individuals that conquered the frontier and built the greatest civilization in history from nothing but blood, sweat and tears. Instead, compared to our ancestors, we have become a whiney, over indulged

---

[7] http://www.heritage.org/Research/Reports/2010/06/The-2010-Index-of-Dependence-on-Government-Dramatic-Spike-in-Dependence-Projected

people who are less capable of providing for our children and ourselves the basic necessities of food and housing.

THE MORAL CONSEQUENCES

Dire economic calamities are not the only problems faced when a nation is gripped by socialism. An over reliance on government for services it should not provide leads to a general devaluation of human life. It all starts when the government begins taking on the role of provider. As we have learned, entitlement programs always grow in scope when left to their own devices. Eventually they grow so large and generous that it becomes more profitable for families to not work and instead live off of government subsidies. It is at this point that the nuclear family begins to breakdown. We all have an inherent need to care and provide for our families. The traditional role of men was of provider, often-sole provider. With the government taking over that role, men become less necessary and turn away from family life often in favor of gangs and crime. It is no coincidence that the decline of the nuclear family began just as state run welfare programs took off.

The nuclear family has been in decline for some time now. In 2001 the New York Times reported that the percentage of married, two parent households was 23.5%. That was down from 25.6% in 1990 and 45% in 1960. The article also noted the number of people living alone is, for the first time, greater than the number of nuclear families. Meanwhile, the number of unmarried couples almost doubled in the last decade of the 20th Century.[8]

This phenomenon is not unique to America either. In England during the same time frame first time marriages dropped from 340,000 in 1971 to only 143,000

---

[8] *The Changing American Family.* May 18, 2001.
http://www.nytimes.com/2001/05/18/opinion/18FRI3.html

in 2007 and the percentage of single mother households quadrupled from 3% in 1961 to 12% in 2009.[9]

This precipitous breakdown in society's most important political unit, the family, inevitably leads to more crime and poverty. In 1995 the Cato Institute's Director of Health and Welfare Studies, Michael Tanner, testified before Congress on how the two correlate. He said:

Welfare contributes to crime in several ways. First, children from single-parent families are more likely to become involved in criminal activity. According to one study, children raised in single-parent families are one-third more likely to exhibit anti-social behavior. Moreover... holding other variables constant, black children from single-parent households are twice as likely to commit crimes as black children from a family where the father is present. Nearly 70 percent of juveniles in state reform institutions come from fatherless homes, as do 43 percent of prison inmates. Research indicates a direct correlation between crime rates and the number of single-parent families in a neighborhood.[10]

Why is testimony from 1995 so important? Because in 1996 a Republican controlled Congress passed and a Democrat President signed into law the most sweeping welfare reform in our nation's history. Of course, the traditional left wing organizations said the legislation would cause more poverty and crime. And of course they were wrong.

A 2001 study examined changes in welfare caseloads and employment from 1983 to 1999. Its analysis showed that in the period after the enactment of welfare reform, policy changes directly related to the 1996 welfare

---

[9] Hannah Richardson. *Nuclear family 'in decline', figures show.* BBC News July 2, 2010. http://www.bbc.co.uk/news/10487318

[10] Testimony of Michael Tanner before the US Senate Subcommittee on Youth Violence. June 7, 1995.

reform accounted for roughly three-quarters of the increase in employment and decrease in dependence.[11] Instead of further eroding the American family and causing more poverty, the 1996 welfare reform law significantly contributed to a decrease in poverty. Poverty among single mothers was cut by one third, to the lowest level in US history and brought to a halt the growth of out-of-wedlock childbearing. The percentage of children living in single-mother families has fallen, and the share living in married couple families has increased, especially among black families.[12]

It may have taken 230 years, but the 1996 welfare reform law vindicated Benjamin Franklin when he said "the more public provisions were made for the poor, the less they provided for themselves, and of course became poorer" and that "the best way of doing good to the poor, is not making them easy in poverty, but leading or driving them out of it".[13]

IS THE FALL OF ROME REPEATING ITSELF?

The Founding Fathers took a keen interest in the republics of antiquity. They often viewed the Greek and Roman republics as man's brightest hour. After all, these were the societies that gave us Socrates, Plato, Aristotle, Cicero and Herodotus. These were the civilizations that gave us democracy, capitalism and feats of engineering not rivaled until the industrial revolution. However, these

---

[11] June E. O'Neill and M. Anne Hill, "Gaining Ground? Measuring the Impact of Welfare Reform on Welfare and Work," Manhattan Institute Civic Report, No. 17, July 2001.

[12] Testimony of Robert Rector before the Subcommittee on Housing and Transportation. Published May 1, 2002.

[13] West, Thomas G. Vindicating the Founders: Race, Sex, Class and Justice in the Origins of America. Rowman and Littlefield. 1997. P.135

great civilizations also collapsed under their own decadence. They collapsed under the weight of great societies that forgot how to be great. Eventually the ancient Romans and Greeks, as societies, became lazy. The people stopped relying on their own ingenuity and started relying on government to solve their problems. Eventually they even abandoned their great republican institutions for despotism so that the government could do even more.

The Founding Fathers saw an important warning for America in the events that led to the collapse of the ancient republics and designed our government to hold back the forces that destroyed them. Unfortunately history is beginning to repeat itself.

One of the first historians to really analyze the fall of Rome was Edward Gibbons, a British contemporary of the Founding Fathers. He published his most famous work *The History of the Decline and Fall of the Roman Empire,* serendipitously, in 1776 and the Founders were certainly well versed in the book by the time they wrote the Constitution.

In his analysis, Gibbons argued that Rome fell as a result of the gradual loss of civic virtue among the populace. The decline in civic virtue was brought on by the outsourcing of civic duties, such as using barbarians to defend Rome instead of maintaining an army. The people became "effeminate", unwilling to live the martial lifestyle that characterized the successes of the early republic. Does this sound at all like the America of today? I certainly think it does.

Take, for example, the wars of the past nine years. The anti-war left has been using a constant drumbeat of casualties to weaken Americans' resolve for war. We have heard incessantly how thousands of Americans died. Each time the number ran over some multiple of ten we learned of 'grim new milestones' in the war. There is no doubt that this tactic was successful. After all, the entire effort in

Iraq would have been given up in 2006 and concluded to be a failure if not for the brilliant and sober leadership of General David Petreaus.

Nobody wants good Americans to die, but compared to every other war our country has waged, Operations Enduring Freedom and Iraqi Freedom have been relatively bloodless. As of October 4th, 2010 a combined 5729 American servicemen and DoD civilians were killed in the two theaters of war[14]. Compare that to World War One's 116,516 deaths or World War Two's 405,399 deaths over much shorter periods.[15] Yet, despite such horrific numbers America successfully waged war in two theaters at once and immediately after the peace treaties were signed our grandfathers and great grandfathers were ready to continue the fight with the Berlin Airlift, the Korean War and the Cold War. It is difficult to imagine Americans having the stomach for that level of warfare today. Unfortunately, one day we will face another scenario as dreadful as WWII. I have no doubt our military can prevail, but if the last eight years are any indication, I am not sure our general public retains enough martial vigor to rise to the occasion.

In a 1994 study for the Cato Institute, historian and economist, Bruce Bartlett explained how the left's hated 'laissez faire' capitalism spurred prosperity in ancient Rome, not rivaled until the 20th century:

The first century of our era witnessed a definitely high level of economic prosperity, made possible by exceptionally favorable conditions. Within the framework of the Empire, embracing vast territories in which peace was established and communications were secure, it was

---

[14] DoD casualty report, 4, October 2010.
http://www.defense.gov/news/casualty.pdf
[15] Defense Manpower Data Center, Statistical Information Analysis Division,
http://siadapp.dmdc.osd.mil/
personnel/CASUALTY/WCPRINCIPAL.pdf.

possible for a bourgeoisie to come into being whose chief interests were economic, which maintained a form of economy resting on the old city culture and characterized by individualism and private enterprise, and which reaped all the benefits inherent in such a system. The State deliberately encouraged this activity of the bourgeoisie, both directly through government protection and its liberal economic policy, which guaranteed freedom of action and an organic growth on the lines of "laissez faire, laissez aller," and directly through measures encouraging economic activity.[16]

and how, ultimately it was socialism that brought down the Roman Empire:

The fall of Rome was fundamentally due to economic deterioration resulting from excessive taxation, inflation, and over-regulation. Higher and higher taxes failed to raise additional revenues because wealthier taxpayers could evade such taxes while the middle class-- and its taxpaying capacity--were exterminated. Although the final demise of the Roman Empire in the West (its Eastern half continued on as the Byzantine Empire) was an event of great historical importance, for most Romans it was a relief.[17]

Rome's confiscatory taxation was brought on by a need to maintain a large, expeditionary army and to pay for the ever-growing social welfare programs instituted by the various emperors. At its peak 320,000 Romans were receiving free grain, but eventually that wasn't good enough and the state began handing out free bread. Eventually, in the 3rd century free oil was added to the dole and occasionally free pork and wine were distributed

---

[16] Bartlett, Bruce. *How Excessive Government Killed Ancient Rome*. The Cato Journal vol 4, # 2, Fall 1994.
[17] Ibid.

to the masses.[18] Even in ancient Rome entitlement programs could not be stopped from growing. They just grew and grew until the whole system collapsed. Remember a few pages back when I said Americans are 14 times more dependent on government now than in 1962? Where does it stop? Last time social welfare was attempted on the scale we see today it ended with the beginning of the Dark Ages.

---

[18] Ibid

Chapter 2
The Nature of Rights

What are rights? This is the most fundamental question we can ask in political science, because the answers to all other questions flow from those three words. This has never been an easy question to answer, but it was considerably easier to answer in the 18th Century.

Why was it easier? Today the answer is confused and contorted with 'wants'. Whenever someone tries to justify a selfish action they claim they have a right to do it. How often have we heard 'I have a right to go to a restaurant without smelling someone else's smoke', 'I have a right to choose' or 'I have a right marry whomever I wish'? Does one really have a right to go to a smoke-free restaurant, kill their unborn child and engage in same-sex marriage or do they simply want to do these things? What about the restaurateur's right to run his business, his property, as he sees fit? Where does the unborn child's right to life fit in to the equation? And what of society's right to define the institution of marriage according to the religious precepts upon which it is built.

So where does one begin? How about with the most eloquent summation of the subject ever written by the hand of man?

We hold these truths to be self-evident, that all men are created equal, that they are endowed by their Creator with certain unalienable rights, that among these are life, liberty and the pursuit of happiness. That to secure these rights, governments are instituted among men, deriving their just powers from the consent of the governed...

In this simple paragraph Thomas Jefferson has given us all the criteria we need to determine what our rights really are. First, that we are all equal. This means that we are all conceived with every right we will ever have and that no person's rights can ever rise above the rights of another. It also means that rights are not a collective gift, as many modern liberals would have you believe. Rights are individual in nature. Second, our Creator endows us with these rights. This is perhaps the most important portion. It lays the foundation of the inalienable nature of our rights. Government does not bestow our rights and they are not derived from the consent of the governed. They are a gift from God and no one else. They are his alone to give and take. Additionally, I enjoy this particular line, because it serves as a poignant rebuttal to all those pseudo-intellectuals out there who try to claim Jefferson was an atheist.

Jefferson goes on to list perhaps the three most famous rights of all: life, liberty and the pursuit of happiness. While this is not an all-inclusive list it does neatly summarize what I think of as the three basic categories of rights; those that enable us to live, those that enable us to live free of coercion from another, or according to the dictates of our own conscience, and those that allow us to thrive emotionally, intellectually and spiritually.

The last part of the paragraph bluntly states that governments are instituted to preserve these rights and derive their power from the governed. While it does not list any additional criteria for what constitutes a right, it does tie together the Natural Law philosophy of the first part with the concept of Social Contract Theory. It is important that these two concepts are side by side in our founding document, because it underscores the fact that government works for the people and not the other way around.

So where does that leave us in our dissection of rights? According to our analysis:

1. Something can only be a right if we are born with it or born with the natural ability to develop it.

2. A right must apply equally to all people as individuals, not as a collective.

3. The exercising of a right cannot, by its very nature, interfere with the rights of another.

4. It is the government's job to protect our rights. We the people empower government to do this by lending some of our liberty, but only within a narrow context and only with our expressed consent.

Before we begin applying these four criteria to today's arguments I think it is worth taking a look at what other Founding Fathers thought of rights. Not surprisingly most, if not all, of the major figures agreed with Jefferson. For example, when George Mason penned the 1776 Virginia Declaration of Rights he wrote:

That all men are by nature equally free and independent, and have certain inherent rights, of which, when they enter into a state of society, they cannot, by any compact, deprive or divest their posterity; namely, the enjoyment of life and liberty, with the means of acquiring and possessing property, and pursuing and obtaining happiness and safety.[19]

---

[19] Article 1 of the Virginia Declaration of Rights, 1776

Though Mason's prose may lack the polished brilliance of Jefferson's (to be fair Jefferson had Benjamin Franklin and John Adams assisting him), all of the same philosophical tenets are there and it goes the extra step of addressing the role of property in the maintenance of rights. The right to pursue and own property cannot be understated. In order to do that subject justice we will come back to it in a later chapter.

A RIGHT ONLY EXISTS IF WE ARE BORN WITH IT OR THE ABILITY TO DEVELOP IT

The Founding Fathers and their philosophical predecessors summed up this idea far more eloquently than I can; we are all born with every right we will ever have and must cede some of them so the government can do things for us that we are not capable of doing for ourselves. They called it the social contract.

Writing as Publius in Federalist #2, John Jay expresses the social contract as "Nothing is more certain than the indispensable necessity of government...that whenever and however it is instituted, the people must cede to it some of their natural rights in order to vest it with requisite powers." Government in turn uses those rights we cede to protect the ones we retain and can't reasonably protect on our own. For this reason Thomas Paine wrote that "government, even in its best state is but a necessary evil; in its worst state an intolerable one."[20]

In his singularly brilliant thesis on the Founding Fathers, *Vindicating the Founders*, Thomas G. West observes how natural law affects the existence of rights. He notes that although the Constitution says we have a right to life and liberty it does not say we have a right to

---

[20] Paine, Thomas. *Common Sense*. Pg 1

happiness, only to the right to pursue happiness. We are born with life and liberty, but we are not born happy nor are we born wealthy. We are simply born with the ability to acquire these things. As such it can be said that we do not have the right to happiness and property only to the right to acquire these things.[21]

RIGHTS APPLY EQUALLY TO ALL PEOPLE AS INDIVIDUALS

The Unites States of America came into being near the end of the Age of Enlightenment. The Declaration of Independence and the Constitution are in many ways the culmination of hundreds of years of philosophical debate as to the exact nature of the rights of man.

It is important to understand the context of the times. During the Enlightenment, the Renaissance's rebirth of classical philosophies mixed with stunning new advances in the physical sciences. Its was an exciting time when men like Sir Isaac Newton were beginning to discover and understand the basic laws of nature. At the same time the philosophers of the day believed they could distill human behavior into universal truths that would apply equally to all people regardless of their station in life. They called this natural law and it formed the basis of civilization. We will focus on the two basic schools of thought. Doing so is, of course a gross simplification of the subject, but is necessary considering the scope of this book.

The Founding Fathers were exposed to incredibly diverse philosophical views including those of Plato, Aristotle, Cicero, Francis Bacon, Martin Luther, John Calvin, Rene Descartes, Montesquieu and Voltaire just to name a few. However, one man's views ascended above

---

[21] West, Thomas G. *Vindicating the Founders: Race, Sex, Class and Justice in the Origins of America.* Rowman and Littlefield. 1997.

all the rest in the hearts of our forefathers. Because his philosophical writings held such sway during the founding, John Locke can rightly be described as the grandfather of America even though he died before our oldest Founding Father, Benjamin Franklin, was even a twinkle in his father's eye. For the purposes of comparison we will also look at what I believe to be the polar opposite of Locke's views, those of Thomas Hobbes.

Thomas Hobbes saw the world as governed exclusively by the use of force. His was a brutish world where kings were instituted to repress the passions of man. John Locke, however, postulated that man's natural state was one of unrestrained freedom and society was created by man's reason to make his interactions with other men easier and more fruitful. Be very glad it was Locke's view of the world that won out.

Hobbes was one of the most outspoken proponents of absolute monarchy. He taught that the most important equality was man's equal ability to kill each other. Thus, civil society depends on the sovereign having "the power of life and death over his subjects."[22] This view stems from Hobbes' belief that man's natural state was one of continual war where our needs and passions will always push us to violence unless otherwise restrained.

We hear echoes of Hobbes' philosophy in the modern big government liberal agenda. The big government, nanny state liberal believes that people are so badly governed by their basest desires that without government coercion greed would prevent the needy from rising above poverty, that the sick would be denied care for want of money and blatant racism would prevent hard working minorities from improving their station in life. Why else would they subject our republic to such ill-

---

[22] Strauss, Leo and Cropsey, Joseph. *History of Political Philosophy 3rd ed.* University of Chicago press 1987. P 399-416.

advised and easily discredited public policies as minimum wages, socialized medicine and affirmative action? What is the Patient Protection and Affordable Care Act (often referred to as Obamacare) if it is not the government's power of life and death over all of us?

John Locke took a very different view of man's natural state. Though he acknowledged the possibility of Hobbes' state of war in nature he saw man's natural state as "men living together according to reason, without a common superior on Earth with authority to judge between them".[23] According to Locke individuals can be trusted to interact with each other in a civil and mutually beneficial manner and government should only intercede when force (violence, theft, etc.) is applied in an unjust manner.

THE MODERN NOTION OF RIGHTS AND THE PURSUIT OF HAPPINESS

During the late 19th and early 20th Centuries a political movement known as Progressivism took root. To be sure, some good came out of the Progressive movement such as women's suffrage, child labor laws and our national parks system. However, progressive reformers performed a terrible injustice for America that we are still trying to cope with today. They redefined America's view of rights. It is my thesis that, although imperfect in execution, the founding documents are perfect in their general philosophy. Therefore any departure from the founding philosophy is inherently wrong.

The major problem with the way rights were redefined was the focus on equality of results. The Founding Fathers understood that we are all created equal, but we do not all end up equal. The choices we make largely determine the paths of our lives. Because of this

---

[23] Ibid. p.478

fact, ensuring equality of results invariably leads to the denial of everyone's rights in favor of the comforts of a few.

It is hard to decipher exactly where we went wrong as a nation, but I think it was with the presidency of Franklin Delano Roosevelt. Excellent arguments can be made for placing the starting point anywhere between the presidencies of Theodore Roosevelt and Woodrow Wilson. They succeeded in bringing about a great many number of changes. Some, like the national parks system, have dramatically improved our country. Other changes, like the ill-conceived sixteenth amendment that made income taxes constitutional, were terrible.

However, I choose to focus on the presidency of FDR, because while previous progressives may have changed various laws and tax codes, FDR succeeded in altering the very fabric of our society. Under him everything changed. Income taxes were raised to punitively high levels. Social Security alienated the need for family in our social safety net and social welfare programs began to replace men as the breadwinners for poor families causing the breakdown of the nuclear family.

On January 11, 1944 FDR presented his State of the Union Address to Congress. During the speech he declared that the political freedoms set forth by our Founding Fathers "proved inadequate to assure us equality in the pursuit of happiness" and "true individual freedom cannot exist without economic security and independence."[24] That may sound like high-minded idealism at first glance, but in reality those statements are stomach-turning regurgitations of Marxist social theories. In order to fix imaginary problems in America's basic framework FDR proposed a *Second Bill of Rights*. These new 'rights' were:

---

[24] http://www.fdrlibrary.marist.edu/archives/address_text.html

The right to a useful and remunerative job in the industries or shops or farms or mines of the nation

The right to earn enough to provide adequate food and clothing and recreation

The right of every farmer to raise and sell his products at a return which will give him and his family a decent living

The right of every businessman, large and small, to trade in an atmosphere of freedom from unfair competition and domination by monopolies at home or abroad

The right of every family to a decent home

The right to adequate medical care and the opportunity to achieve and enjoy good health

The right to adequate protection from the economic fears of old age, sickness, accident, and unemployment

The right to a good education

FDR's new rights immediately conflict with the fundamental nature of rights as handed down to us by the Founders. There are several reasons, but the most glaring is on the emphasis on equality of results.

Does everyone really have the right to "a useful and remunerative job" and "a decent home"? What about those too lazy to work? Why would a farmer have a right to sell his products at a rate that provides a decent living if that would conflict with the customer's right to pay a fair market price?

Roosevelt's 'rights' are good things, indeed, but they are not rights. If they were rights, government would be required to take *active* measures to secure them per man's agreement with society through the social contract. Unfortunately, doing so would require government to deny the rights of others. Perhaps Alexander Hamilton in Federalist #10 handed down the best explanation of the tension between equality of results and liberty to us.

The diversity in the faculties of men, from which the rights of property originate, is not less an insuperable obstacle to a uniformity of interests. The protection of these faculties is the first object of government. From the protection of different and unequal faculties of acquiring property, the possession of different degrees and kinds of property immediately results; and from the influence of these on the sentiments and views of the respective proprietors, ensues a division of the society into different interests and parties.

Hamilton begins this passage by linking the "diversity of faculties" in each of us with our inherent property rights. In this Jefferson agreed when he wrote that we have a right to *pursue* happiness. Essentially what they are saying is we have the right to as much property as we can amass, but not a single penny more than our talent and work ethic will allow us to attain on our own. I marvel at the genius of these men, as they were able to refute our entire modern day social welfare system with just one sentence each.

Hamilton goes on to say that government's job is, first and foremost, to protect these unequal abilities to acquire property and in doing so some people will naturally become rich while others will not. It is not government's job to ensure everyone is rich or even well fed. Instead it must ensure that we retain the freedom to become so through our own hard work and ingenuity. Then and only then can our rights be secured.

FDR did get a couple of things right in his rhetoric. When he said every businessman, large and small, has a right to "trade in an atmosphere of freedom from unfair competition and domination by monopolies at home or abroad" and that each of us has a right o a good education he was espousing exactly what our Founding Fathers believed. Unfortunately his execution and the execution of those who followed ruined any hope of applying these principles in a manner consistent with the proper maintenance of a republic.

It goes without saying that when our creator endowed us with the right to pursue happiness he did so with the understanding that we were all granted this on an equal basis. However, we can't truly pursue happiness if we are subject to unfair monopolies. Adam Smith's *An Inquiry into the Nature and Causes of the Wealth of Nations* was hugely influential in guiding the course the Founding Fathers set us on. He taught that the welfare of a nation and its wealth (annual national product) are inseparable with the sum of each individual's labor contributing to that wealth. Since each individual has an underlying interest in maximizing his wealth, creating the freest possible atmosphere to pursue these goals will produce the greatest amount of wealth and thus the greatest amount of happiness for society.[25]

What Roosevelt and modern day liberals do not understand is that there is no worse monopoly than the US Federal Government. If a corporation becomes a monopoly it can deny us our right only through unfair business practices, but the government can do that and use the force of law to deny us our rights. Worse still is the idea that this can be a good thing; an idea embraced by our current government.

One of President Obama's most influential advisors, Cass Sunstein believes that private property and economic value are not natural occurrences, but instead

---

[25] Strauss, Leo and Cropsey, Joseph. *History of Political Philosophy 3rd ed.* University of Chicago press 1987. P 649.

are created by government and law. He goes on to say that it is government's job to redistribute wealth.[26] This is communism in its most naked form and it is a sad testimony to the values of a president who would allow himself counsel from such a man. That he would encourage the debasement of our national discourse with such ideas should horrify all Americans.

Roosevelt, Sunstein, Obama and liberals in general show their ignorance on another account. Large cookie cutter government programs do not maximize our ability to pursue happiness. In 1965 when President Johnson began his war on poverty our Federal Government spent less than $9 billion (1.3 percent of GDP) annually on poverty relief. By 1993 that figure had ballooned to almost $325 billion (5 percent of GDP) annually.[27] A 3600% increase in spending should have corresponded to at least some reduction in poverty right? Wrong. In 1969 federal family income estimates showed about 12% of Americans lived in poverty. By 1997 that number hovered around 15%[28] If an additional $314 billion dollars in federal spending corresponds to a 3% increase in poverty, then what amount are we to believe will actually reduce the problem. Liberals are too blinded by ideological stubbornness to see that paying people to be poor only encourages more poverty.

Benjamin Franklin understood this though:

In my youth I traveled much, and I observed in different countries, that the more public provisions were made for the poor, the less they provided for themselves, and of course became poorer. And, on the contrary, the

---

[26] Levin, Mark. *Liberty and Tyranny*. Simon and Schuster. 2009 p.44

[27] West, Thomas G. Vindicating the Founders: Race, Sex, Class and Justice in the Origins of America. Rowman and Littlefield. 1997. P.143

[28] Ibid. p. 139

less was done for them, the more they did for themselves and became richer.[29]

Caleb Strong, a lawyer and governor of Massachusetts who assisted John Adams in drafting the Massachusetts Constitution and Madison draft the US Constitution, agreed. He noted that:

[Inequality] arises from the nature of things, and not from any defect in the form of administration of government. All that the best government can do is prevent that inequality which fraud, oppression or violence would produce.[30]

John Adams concurred:

The moment the idea is admitted into society that property is not as sacred as the laws of God, and that there is not a force of law and public justice to protect it, anarchy and tyranny commence. If `Thou shalt not covet' and `Thou shalt not steal' were not commandments of Heaven, they must be made inviolable precepts in every society before it can be civilized or made free.[31]

Even well over 200 years ago the failure of a paternalist national government was evident to our Founding Fathers.

---

[29] Ibid. p. 135

[30] Flynn, Daniel. *Why the Left Hates America: Exposing the Lies that have Obscured Our Nation's Greatness.* Prima Publishing. 2002. P. 205

[31] John Adams, A Defense of the American Constitutions, 1787

Chapter 3
The Founders and Religion

Please read this chapter carefully. I believe it may be the most important of the book. How often have you heard an argument that included the phrase "right and wrong according to whom" and that religion has no place whatsoever in the political sphere? Essentially this is an argument for moral relativism and it is perhaps the most dangerous philosophy ever espoused by its unwitting proponents.

What was one of the first things all the worst tyrants of the 20th century did after taking power? Lenin, Stalin, Hitler, Mao, Pot, etc. all banned religion. Why did they ban religion? They banned it, because religion creates moral certainty. When you read John Locke, Adam Smith and Edmund Burke you'll see that our Founding Fathers understood this and believed religion had to be central to the public and private lives of a republic's citizens. They realized that moral relativism was the key to allowing tyranny to flourish, because it allowed anyone to justify anything. When ethics are relative, anything can be ethical.

If you think that right and wrong are subject to one's point of view then in order to be intellectually consistent you must also believe that from Hitler's point of view the Holocaust was right and we have no right to judge his actions. Of course it wasn't and of course no reasonable observer believes that. With that in mind, anyone who claims to be a moral relativist is actually just a run of the mill a hypocrite.

Without moral certainty there is no higher authority than the state. Our founding documents clearly state that our rights come from God. This means only He can give or take rights away from us. In almost every other country this is not the case. The state is the highest authority. The result is 100 million people killed by Communism in the 20th Century and over a billion more enslaved.[32]

The moral certainty religion creates prevents the populace from embracing the radical ideologies of dictators and provides an important check on the power of the state. Perhaps this is why Raisa Gorbachev, wife of the former communist dictator, wrote her PhD dissertation on the USSR's need for government run daycare. She argued that without state run daycare too many children would be left home with their religious grandparents as their parents went to work.[33]

THE RELIGIONS OF THE FOUNDERS

Today, far too many revisionist historians disregard the religious beliefs of the Founding Fathers. They are, in this respect, completely wrong. During his famous travels through America, Alexis de Tocqueville observed "there is no country in the world where the Christian religion retains a greater influence over the souls of men than in America."[34] Tocqueville witnessed what we have forgotten over time: that the Founding Fathers and their generation were a deeply religious group. Their

---

[32] Bennett, William J. America: The Last Best Hope.p529 Nashville, TN. 2007

[33] Ibid, p.507

[34] Tocqueville. Democracy in America: Vol 1. P.304

beliefs were as much informed by Jesus and Mosses, as they were Locke and Smith.

Today we are often taught that the overarching religious belief of the Founding Fathers was Deism, a system of thought advocating natural religion, emphasizing morality, and in the 18th century denying the interference of the Creator with the laws of the universe.[35] To a certain extent, for a few Founders this is true. The problem is this revisionist view of the Founders is largely limited to Benjamin Franklin and Thomas Jefferson and even in their cases it is not entirely factual. I have even heard otherwise intelligent people argue that Jefferson was an atheist. Can it really be true that the man who penned the most stirring appeals to the divine nature of our rights was an atheist? No, this notion is false.

I clearly remember being taught in high school that Franklin was a Deist. I can even recall conversations with some of my ill-informed friends who repeat this big lie. However, it was Franklin who motioned that the Constitutional Convention open with a prayer and it was Franklin who said "the longer I live, the more convincing proofs I see of this truth--that God governs in the affairs of men." and "without His concurring aid, we shall succeed in this political building no better than the builders of Babel."[36] If a deist is indeed someone who denies God's interference with the affairs of man then Franklin was no Deist. Or at the very least, the vast accumulated wisdom of his many years caused him to abandon such beliefs in old age.

Now, if I leave you with that one quote from Franklin to support my thesis then I would be no better than the revisionist historians and ill-informed liberals who argue the opposite. The truth is Franklin was far too complicated to fit into a neat little category. He was the

---

[35] Online reference: http://www.merriam-webster.com/dictionary/deist

[36] http://www.loc.gov/exhibits/religion/rel06.html

quintessential renaissance man. In his autobiography Franklin lists among the reasons he left Boston in 1723 that his "indiscrete disputations about religion began to make [him] pointed at with horror by good people as an infidel and atheist".[37] As a young man he appeared deeply skeptical of traditional religions, but it is interesting that he refers to as "good people" the church going members of Boston who accused him of being an atheist. To me this implies that he was not only wounded by others viewing him as an atheist, but that even if he did not explicitly subscribe to any one religion he understood that a belief in God was essential to being a good person.

At one point in his life, Franklin sought to improve himself morally by listing several virtues and keeping a daily record of how well he performed. 13th on this list was humility, which he described as imitating Jesus and Socrates.[38] He makes no reference to listing the virtues in order of importance, but it is significant that he places Jesus and Socrates together in the description. It shows that during a time when he was supposedly a Deist and should have cared little about the life of Jesus he actually viewed him as a role model to be revered in the same breath as the philosophical founder of Western Civilization. Clearly we cannot look into the heart of any man and especially not one as complicated as Franklin, but what he has left us is a portrait of a skeptical young man with deep respect for religion who grew into an old man who believed in a more conventional and Christian view of God. Though, to classify him as any particular sect of Christianity would be disingenuous.

Jefferson is an equally difficult nut to crack. Was he a Christian? Not in the strict sense often used today. Was he an atheist? Absolutely not! Just read the Declaration of Independence and it is obvious that he

---

[37] Autobiography of Benjamin Franklin Ch. 1

[38] ibid p. 105

believed in God. Delving further into his life and works it becomes clear that he was no Evangelical Christian and he did not believe in the supernatural aspects of the Bible. However, is it necessary to believe, literally, every word of the Bible to consider yourself a Christian? I believe Jefferson would have said no and I believe Jefferson considered himself a Christian. Why? Because he said he was.

My views...are the result of a life of inquiry and reflection, and very different from the anti-Christian system imputed to me by those who know nothing of my opinions. To the corruptions of Christianity I am, indeed, opposed; but not to the genuine precepts of Jesus Himself. I am a Christian, in the only sense in which He wished any one to be: sincerely attached to His doctrines, in preference to all others; ascribing to Himself every human excellence; and believing He never claimed any other.[39]

Of course even that definitive statement, by the man himself does not end the debate. To be honest I don't have a simple answer to the question of Jefferson's religion, but neither did he. So the next few paragraphs will use some of his quotes to present both sides of the argument. I will leave the rest to you.

Take for example this quote from Jefferson's *Notes on Virginia*:

Difference of opinion is advantageous in religion. The several sects perform the office of a censor morum over each other. Is uniformity attainable? Millions of innocent men, women, and children, since the introduction of Christianity, have been burnt, tortured, fined, imprisoned; yet we have not advanced one inch toward

---

[39] Thomas Jefferson, letter to Dr. Benjamin Rush, Apr. 21, 1803

*uniformity. What has been the effect of coercion? To make
one-half the world fools, and the other half hypocrites.*[40]

At first blush this would seem to be a damning
indictment of Christianity, but keep in mind two things.
First, in the 18th Century even the most enlightened men
had little experience beyond Christianity so the words
religion and Christianity were probably interchangeable in
the general discourse. Second, he is not speaking on the
tenets of Christianity per se. Rather he is commenting on
the results of differences between the various sects created
by men. The more one honestly studies Jefferson's
thoughts on religion, the clearer it becomes that he
diverged not from the teachings of Jesus, but from the
teachings of the churches. A letter to John Adams a little
more than two years before their deaths reads:

*The truth is, that the greatest enemies to the
doctrines of Jesus are those, calling themselves the
expositors of them, who have perverted them for the
structure of a system of fancy absolutely
incomprehensible, and without any foundation in His
genuine words.*[41]

When viewed in the larger context of official
documents he wrote, such as the Declaration of
Independence, and the more intimate letters written to
friends I think it becomes a little clearer that Jefferson
viewed himself as a pious man. Though, he considered
himself a sect unto himself. He clearly revered the
teachings of Jesus, but reviled the church structures
created by men. He felt that they served the purpose of
enriching men rather than preaching the word of God. In
this way, the Founding Father most often portrayed as a

---

[40] http://www.notable-quotes.com/r/religion_quotes_ii.html
[41] Thomas Jefferson, letter to John Adams, Apr. 11, 1823

deist or atheist actually bears more resemblance to religious figures like Martin Luther.

And what about the other Founding Fathers? Our first two presidents were very religious. George Washington was an Episcopal vestryman, and John Adams described himself as "a church going animal."[42] Washington referred to religion as the source of morality in his farewell address and "a necessary spring of popular government," while Adams asserted men "may plan and speculate for Liberty, but it is religion and morality alone, which can establish the principles upon which freedom can securely stand."[43]

A WALL OF SEPARATION?

Perhaps no issue has been more convoluted and confounded than the issue of separation of church and state. Many people, usually on the left, have been preaching with religious zeal that we must have no religion in government and that was the way the Founders intended it. This simply is not true. Nor is it true that all the Founders wanted an intimate relationship between the two.

Most of the confusion relates to Jefferson's letter to the Danbury Baptists in 1802 where the term 'wall of separation of church and state' was coined. The next page contains the full, edited version that was printed in the newspapers of the time.

---

[42] http://www.notable-quotes.com/r/religion_quotes_ii.html
[43] ibid

Gentlemen

The affectionate sentiments of esteem and approbation which you are so good as to express towards me, on behalf of the Danbury Baptist association, give me the highest satisfaction. My duties dictate a faithful and zealous pursuit of the interests of my constituents, & in proportion as they are persuaded of my fidelity to those duties, the discharge of them becomes more and more pleasing.

Believing with you that religion is a matter which lies solely between Man & his God, that he owes account to none other for his faith or his worship, that the legitimate powers of government reach actions only, & not opinions, I contemplate with sovereign reverence that act of the whole American people which declared that their legislature should "make no law respecting an establishment of religion, or prohibiting the free exercise thereof," thus building a wall of separation between Church & State. Adhering to this expression of the supreme will of the nation in behalf of the rights of conscience, I shall see with sincere satisfaction the progress of those sentiments which tend to restore to man all his natural rights, convinced he has no natural right in opposition to his social duties.

I reciprocate your kind prayers for the protection & blessing of the common father and creator of man, and tender you for yourselves & your religious association, assurances of my high respect & esteem.

Th JeffersonJan. 1. 1802.[44]

We must keep two things in mind when reading this letter. First, Jefferson was not a signatory to the Constitution. He was not even in the country when the Constitution was created. He was the ambassador to France at the time. Though he was unquestionably one of

---

[44] http://www.loc.gov/loc/lcib/9806/danpre.html

the most influential Founding Fathers, he should not be the final word on the content of the Constitution since he was not a participant of the debates. Unfortunately that is exactly what the Supreme Court did in the 1878 case of *Reynolds v. United States* when they declared "that it may be accepted almost as an authoritative declaration of the scope and effect of the [first] amendment." This misapplication of jurisprudence was again used in 1947 and the 1948 case of *McCollum v. Board of Education.*[45]

The Supreme Court's constant reliance Jefferson's metaphor represents one of the most egregious and lazy misuses of jurisprudence in our history for three reasons. First, the phrase "wall of separation of church and state" appears nowhere in the Constitution. Second, it ascribes beliefs that not all the signers of the Constitution shared. Third, and I am repeating this for effect, Jefferson was not at the Constitutional Convention. He was a brilliant philosopher and we are all in his debt for his work on the Declaration of Independence, but his opinions should not hold the same weight as George Washington, James Madison, Alexander Hamilton and Benjamin Franklin. Even the lesser-known Framers like Gouverneur Morris, Rufus King and John Rutledge deserve a higher place in interpreting the Constitution, because they were actually there.

The Supreme Court performed a great disservice to the country by cherry picking one phrase from which to inform their views. In doing so they lowered the intellectual bar for all legal justifications. A deeper analysis of the views of the Framers could have yielded the same results without compromising the intellectual integrity of the court system. Ironically, it could have also yielded the opposite results. Take for example the views of the two men I regard as the most important

---

[45] http://www.loc.gov/loc/lcib/9806/danbury.html

Founding Fathers, James Madison and George Washington. Madison's views were much closer to those of Jefferson and modern day protagonists of the wall of separation. Washington on the other hand not only believed in a much closer relationship between church and state, but also practiced it.

Madison vetoed seven bills during his tenure as President of the United States; three of which he vetoed on the grounds they violated the Establishment Clause of the Constitution. The 11th Congress sent him two bills, HR 155 and HR 170 that provided for "incorporating the Protestant Episcopal Church in the town of Alexandria, in the District of Columbia" and "for the relief of Richard Tervin... and the Baptist Church at Salem meeting house, in the Mississippi Territory" respectfully. The 14th Congress sent him HR 106 which was to "provide for the free importation of stereotype plates and to encourage the printing and gratuitous distribution of the Scriptures by the Bible Societies with in the United States".[46]

Clearly Madison viewed almost any intercourse between the federal government and individual religious institutions as a violation of the establishment clause of the Constitution. This view is consistent with Jefferson's view and the prevailing interpretation of the First Amendment with respect to the US Congress. Madison, like Jefferson believed that keeping political and religious institutions insulated from each other actually worked to the benefit of both.

George Washington, on the other hand, embraced religion as an integral part of a republican society. One of his most important contributions to religious inclusion in the political sphere was his Oct 3, 1789 proclamation of a day of Thanksgiving. In it he designated Thursday, Nov 26, 1789 as a day "to be devoted by the People of these States to the service of that great and glorious Being, who

---

[46] http://www.senate.gov/reference/Legislation/Vetoes/Presidents/MadisonJ.pdf

is the beneficent Author of all the good that was, that is, or that will be" and "and also that we may then unite in most humbly offering our prayers and supplications to the great Lord and Ruler of Nations and beseech him to pardon our national and other transgressions--to enable us all, whether in public or private stations, to perform our several and relative duties properly and punctually".[47]

In a 1785 letter to his neighbor, George Mason, Washington professed that he was not alarmed by a bill under consideration that would have required citizen to pay a tax to religious institutions of the faith they professed. He appears unbothered by the use of government authority to support religious institutions, but did not support the bill, because he believed it divisive and "impolitic" for government to broach the subject.[48]

Since Washington wrote this letter before the Constitution was ratified and in a personal capacity it obviously does not have the same effect on legal precedent that Madison's vetoes or Jefferson's letter to the Danbury Baptists should. However, it is an intriguing look into just how intimately the father of our country believed government and religion should interact. It is important that our modern views be informed not only by the official writings of our Founding Fathers, but also their personal views.

I am not advocating either side. That will come later in the chapter. What I want is for you to ask yourself this question: If the father of our country and the father of our government can be so diametrically opposed in their views of the first amendment as it relates to religious freedom then who are we to build an entire legal framework around a single quote?

---

[47] http://gwpapers.virginia.edu/documents/thanksgiving/transcript.html
[48] http://memory.loc.gov/mss/mgw/mgw2/012/2440242.jpg

HOW DOES THIS APPLY TODAY?

Of course everything you have read so far is academic unless we apply it to the issues of the day. Court cases involving religious freedom spend a great deal of time on the front pages of our newspapers and are often the subject of endless debate among the pundits and talking heads on TV.

So whom should we side with? Is Washington and his intricately woven relationship between Christianity and government right or is Madison correct with his vision of a government completely independent of religion? The short answer is neither... and both. The long answer is as follows.

What is so often missing from the debate is the acknowledgment that society and government are two separate entities, but it is the job of government officials to represent both. The President, for example is both the head of state and the head of government. Many countries, such as England, split these duties between two people. The King and Queen are the heads of state and their Prime Minister is the head of the government. In America, one person performs these duties, so often the lines are blurred with respect to what is appropriate.

Washington was right to declare a day of prayer and kiss the bible after taking the oath of office. He was right to invoke God even when signing legislation and addressing Congress, because in this capacity he was acting as the head of state. He was acting as the leader of a very religious people. He was misguided in supporting the idea that government should levy taxes to support religious establishments.

Madison was wrong to think there should be no intercourse between government and religion, because of the fact that government officials must sometimes act as heads of state. However, he was right to deny the granting of federal funds to build churches as that is a clear case of government establishing religion even if only regionally.

To find the answer we should read and apply the First Amendment as the Framers intended. Literally. The relevant portion reads: "Congress shall make no law respecting an establishment of religion, or prohibiting the free exercise thereof..." However, we must also consider the Tenth Amendment which reads: "The powers not delegated to the United States by the Constitution, nor prohibited by it to the States, are reserved to the States respectively, or to the people".

When we read these two amendments together we get the whole picture. The First Amendment prohibits *Congress* i.e. the Federal Government from making any laws that would establish religion. It does not prohibit the sort of overt religious sentiment demonstrated by Washington. The Tenth Amendment reserves to the states and the people any powers not given to the Federal Government or explicitly prohibited to them. That means that if a city government wants to place a manger scene in the town square at Christmas time or if a judge in Alabama wants to display the Ten Commandments (which are displayed on the façade of the Supreme Court alongside images of other historical law givers) they are within the bounds of the Constitution to do so, because those actions do not prohibit anyone from practicing their religion and do not require the practicing of any particular religion.

In determining the Constitutionality of government's involvement with religion we must ask three questions.

1) Is Congress creating a law that elevates one particular religion above another, essentially establishing a religion?

2) Does the law or government action inhibit individuals from the valid exercising of their religion?

3) Does the law require the personal expression of a religion?

The Constitution gives considerably more leeway to state and local governments in these and almost all matters. That is the heart of federalism. We were given a country where the national government was meant to be small and limited in scope, powerful enough to fight an invading army, but too weak limit the personal expression of one's religion.

At the beginning of this chapter I said it just might be the most important one of the book, because it speaks to the moral bedrock of our nation and our government. The wisdom of the Founders is clear. They understood something that we forgot almost a century ago and are just now relearning. America is a Christian nation, but our government is not. America is a Christian nation, because the majority of her people are Christian and most of their traditions are rooted in Christianity. And even though it was designed to be secular in nature, men with a wide variety of religious views built our government. Some were pious "church going animals" like John and Samuel Adams. Others chose to explore their spirituality in a much more reserved fashion like Thomas Jefferson and James Madison. We should not force religion on anyone, but we remove it from the public domain at our own peril.

Chapter 4
The Founding and Social Welfare

It is a common and dreadful misconception that America in the founding era was a place where rich elites ruled this country totally unconcerned about the welfare of the weakest and most vulnerable members of society. Nothing could be further from the truth. In fact America, prior to the advent of progressivism was far more effective in providing for the poor and downtrodden than it is today.

The Founding Fathers understood that faith, family and charity are infinitely more effective in providing for the poor than any government program could be. However, they also understood that there was a role for government in the process, but that role was almost entirely local.

The wise men that created America understood a fundamental law of nature that we as a civilization have nearly forgotten. If government, especially at the state and federal level, tries to absolve the masses of poverty it will serve only to *increase* the miseries of poverty. This is because it can't do so without violating the basic rights of everyone to subsidize the sloth of a few. Benjamin Franklin summed up the first part of this truism perfectly in an article for the *London Chronicle* in November 1766.

I am for doing good to the poor, but I differ in opinion of the means. I think the best way of doing good to the poor, is not making them easy in poverty, but leading or driving them out of it. In my youth I travelled much, and I observed in different countries, that the more public provisions were made for the poor, the less they provided for themselves, and of course became poorer.[49]

It seems obvious to the thoughtful observer. If you make poverty profitable through subsidies then it will increase. It is also obvious to the thoughtful observer that government cannot subsidize poverty without taxing the success of those who work hard. As Thomas Jefferson so eloquently explained in an 1816 letter:

To take from one, because it is thought his own industry and that of his fathers has acquired too much, in order to spare to others, who, or whose fathers, have not exercised equal industry and skill, is to violate arbitrarily the first principle of association, the guarantee to everyone the free exercise of his industry and the fruits acquired by it.[50]

As Hamlet would say, there in lies the rub. By taking measures to relieve the poor the government only removes the two objects capable of lifting them from poverty; the capital that could be invested in them from the rich and their own hard work.

Poverty and social welfare, like everything else in life, are governed by the same natural laws that govern human nature and economics. Because government derives its power from taking certain rights from the people, it can't help one man without stealing from another. Specifically, it must steal from the rich man (or

[49] West, Thomas G. Vindicating the Founders: Race, Sex, Class and Justice in the Origins of America. Rowman and Littlefield. 1997. P.135

[50] Ibid, p. 136

middle class entrepreneur) who would otherwise trade his money for the poor man's labor, thereby benefiting both. In the end federal involvement in social welfare makes us all poorer.

THE GOVERNMENT'S ROLE

If there is one indisputable fact about how the Founding Fathers intended the Federal Government to operate it is that they wished for it to be as limited as possible, especially in the realm of social justice and welfare. They understood that the Federal Government should have no role whatsoever in remediating poverty. James Madison remarked in the House of Representatives on January 10, 1794:

The government of the United States is a definite government, confined to specified objects. It is not like the state governments, whose powers are more general. Charity is no part of the legislative duty of the government[51]*... I cannot undertake to lay my finger on that article of the Constitution which granted a right to Congress of expending, on objects of benevolence, the money of their constituents.*[52]

It is rare to find such a definitive answer to a historical inquiry, especially from such brilliant and enigmatic men as the Founding Fathers, but Madison in his typical no nonsense academic style gave us just that. Can there be any doubt that all *federal* welfare programs

---

[51] The Debates in the Several State Conventions on the Adoption of the Federal Constitution [Elliot's Debates, Volume 4] On the Memorial of the Relief Committee of Baltimore, for the Relief of St. Domingo Refugees.http://memory.loc.gov/cgi-bin/query/r?ammem/hlaw:@field(DOCID+@lit(ed00423)):

[52] http://memory.loc.gov/cgi-bin/ampage?collId=llac&fileName=004/llac004.db&recNum=82

are unconstitutional and ultimately illegal after reading those comments from the father of our Constitution? Apparently there can be. There was doubt from the very beginning. Take for example this correspondence between James Robertson Jr and James Madison. In letter dated April 3, 1831 Robertson asked Madison:

> *What are we to do with the words "general welfare" in the grant of powers to Congress? I know that the 10th Amendment is relied upon, for the purpose of reducing this latitudinous language, within limited lines; but when the language of that amendment is examined; the doubt does not seem to be removed. "All powers, not delegated, (says the amendment) shall remain with the States or the people; but then the question recurs; is the power, to promote the general welfare, delegated? If it is, then it falls not within the language of the 10th amendment; if it is not delegated; then it does—This is a knotty point.*[53]

Madison responded a couple weeks later by writing:

> *With respect to the words "general welfare" I have always regarded them as qualified by the detail of powers connected with them. To take them in a literal and unlimited sense, would be a metamorphosis of the Constitution into a character, which there is a host of proofs was not contemplated by its creators.*[54]

In this instance, Madison lays out the blueprint for government's role in welfare. The Federal Government

---

[53] Letter from James Robertson Jr to James Madison. 3 Apr 1831.
http://rotunda.upress.virginia.edu/founders/default.xqy?keys=FOEA-search-1-4&expandNote=on#match

[54] Letter from James Madison to James Robertson Jr. 20 Apr 1831.
http://rotunda.upress.virginia.edu/founders/default.xqy?keys=FOEA-print-02-02-02-2332

has no role whatsoever, but the states are empowered to experiment and take more active roles in providing for the general welfare. This is because state and local governments are much closer to the people, geographically and socially.

Thomas Jefferson took a nearly identical view of the federal government's role in the welfare of the people. He said, "if we can but prevent the government from wasting the labors of the people, under the pretence of taking care of them, they must become happy."[55]

This was perhaps, the biggest difference between the new country founded 1776 and the old world they broke with. Over the course of hundreds of years Europeans became accustomed to various aristocracies exercising unlimited power to take care of their needs and wants. The result was overcrowded and poverty stricken cities.

America, by contrast was wild and free. Separated by hundreds, sometimes thousands of miles from their national government, people were forced to take care of their own affairs and to the surprise of none of our Founding Fathers, they always performed better than the government in this capacity. Jefferson succinctly summed up this phenomenon in his first inaugural address:

A wise and frugal Government, which shall restrain men from injuring one another, shall leave them otherwise free to regulate their own pursuits of industry and improvement, and shall not take from the mouth of labor the bread it has earned. This is the sum of good government, and this is necessary to close the circle of our felicities.[56]

---

[55] Letter of Thomas Jefferson to Thomas Cooper Nov. 29, 1802. http://memory.loc.gov/cgi-bin/ampage?collId=mtj1&fileName=mtj1page027.db&recNum=500

[56] Thomas Jefferson's first inaugural address. March 4, 1801. http://avalon.law.yale.edu/19th_century/jefinau1.asp

All of this does not mean that government should have no role in taking care of the poor. It only means the federal government should have no role. In fact, Jefferson helped draft Virginia laws before and after the Revolution that brought local governments into the act of helping the poor.

In his book *Notes On the State of Virginia* Jefferson explained how local parishes used taxpayer money to provide boarding for the poor in the homes of farmers who volunteered to support those unable to support themselves. Essentially a board of 12 vestrymen was responsible for collecting and distributing a tithing to local farmers who in turn used that money to defray the cost of boarding indigent members of the community. Those that had some means of supporting themselves could receive supplemental income or were placed in boarding houses where they would receive lodging, clothing, food and perhaps a marketable skill as long as they provided some labor to the community.[57]

This was considered a standard method for supporting the poor, completely without controversy in those days. In Jefferson's words:

Nearly the same method of providing for the poor prevails through all our states; and from Savannah to Portsmouth you will seldom meet a beggar. In the larger towns indeed they sometimes present themselves. These are usually foreigners, who have never obtained a settlement in any parish. I never yet saw a native American begging in the streets or highways. A subsistence is easily gained here: and if, by misfortunes, they are thrown on the charities of the world, those provided by their own country are so comfortable and so

---

[57] Jefferson, Thomas. *Notes on the State of Virginia.* Query 14, p.259.
http://etext.virginia.edu/etcbin/toccernew2?id=JefVirg.sgm&images=images/mo
deng&data=/texts/english/modeng/parsed&tag=public&part=14&division=div1

certain, that they never think of relinquishing them to become strolling beggars.[58]

In this case the term *native American* refers to those of European decent in America, not the modern definition. However, Jefferson provides us an illustration of how the poor can be well supported through a combination of local government and charitable efforts. This system, long since abandoned by our society was far superior to anything we have today. Today we simply cut the poor a check or provide them with whatever free service they require and forget about them. We give hand out after hand out and wonder why people remain trapped in a cycle of poverty that keeps them coming back for more government subsidies.

During the Founders' time, however, the poor were well supported *and* supervised. No one who was able to work received public funds without contributing to the community and those that were unable to work received personal care from members of the community who had a vested interest in the welfare of their fellow man. It was a system that brought individuals together in support of each other, bringing communities closer. Today we naively believe that our faceless, soulless, bureaucratic method of redistributing wealth is somehow superior. We can't be more wrong.

Since progressivism poisoned our national consciousness with the idea of social justice, it has become commonplace to hear people say things like 'the rich should pay their fair share' or we must 'level the playing field'. If you have ever said something like that, then you are in danger of becoming what the Soviets once called a useful idiot, when referring to American liberals and should immediately consume as much of our Founding Fathers' philosophy as possible.

---

[58] Ibid

One of the greatest expressions of the outright stupidity that is social justice came from then Senator Barrack Obama on the 2008 campaign trail. At a June 9th campaign rally in Raleigh, North Carolina he said "I'll make oil companies like Exxon pay a tax on their windfall profits, and we'll use the money to help families pay for their skyrocketing energy costs and other bills".[59] This statement is either profoundly stupid or profoundly evil. It is stupid, because any economics 101 student can tell you that taxes always raise the cost of business and are always passed on to the consumer in the form of higher costs. Therefore, any government program designed to ease the burden of high commodity prices necessarily *raises* the cost of not only that particular commodity, but also increases the cost of that commodity's derivate products. When one also considers the fact that much, if not most of the money government would give to the poor is wasted in corruption and red tape it becomes obvious that any attempt by government to impose social justice eventually leads to further suffering of the supposedly aggrieved parties.

This statement is evil if, with a complete grasp on the intricacies of free markets, Obama was using it to enflame class discord for personal gain. I have never met the man so I will refrain, in this case, from passing judgment on his motives.

WHAT IS THE INDIVIDUAL'S ROLE?

So who is ultimately responsible for lifting the poor out of poverty? Is it the rich who can easily afford it? Is it society in general? Unless you started reading this book on this page, you know what I am going to say. It is solely the responsibility of the individual.

---

[59] http://www.reuters.com/article/idUSWAT00963020080609

The Founding Fathers intended each person to be the sovereign in their own lives. That is the entire point federal republicanism. Each political level is responsible for only what the lower levels can't perform for themselves. The political hierarchy begins with the individual and families, followed by local governments, the states and then the federal government. Cities and counties are responsible for maintaining police and fire departments. States maintain militias, roads and ensure legal unity among local municipalities. The Federal Government equips and directs the military, negotiates treaties and mediates disputes between the states.

As individuals we can't do those things for ourselves. Social contract theory tells us that we agree to cede some of our rights to the government so it can be empowered to do them for us. We retain the rights and thus the responsibilities inherent in everything else in our lives. Since we are fully capable as individuals of earning money and procuring food, housing, medical care, and luxury items we, as individuals, are solely responsible for them. Government's responsibility is simply to facilitate our pursuit of those things, not give them to us.

We all understand that individuals and government each have roles to play in society. Similarly, even like-minded people differ on some of the specifics: the who, what, when, where and how. Unfortunately, what modern day socialists can't comprehend is the *why*? Take for example the book *Nudge* written by Obama advisor Cass Sunstein and economist Richard Thaler. The premise of this freighting decent into what the authors call libertarian paternalism (yet another term to describe socialism) is that:

Many people who favor freedom of choice reject any kind of paternalism...The false assumption is that almost all people, almost all of the time, make choices that are in their best interest or at the very least are better than the choices that would be made by someone else.[60]

To Thaler and Sunstein individuals are inherently incapable of making the best choices for themselves and by extension society. Therefore it is incumbent upon government and corporations to provide a limited number of choices for the individual. Because the choices are pre-screened by supposedly more intelligent bureaucrats and captains of industry, individuals are less likely to screw things up.

They, and all socialists like them are completely missing the point of a free society. We reject their nonsense, not because we believe that individuals will make better choices, but because the individual's right to make his or her own decisions is a gift granted by God through free will. If people make bad choices like smoking or over eating so be it. As long as they are not hurting anyone else, they have that right.

So whom would our Founding Fathers agree with? Cass or me? Well...

I would rather be exposed to the inconveniencies attending too much liberty than those attending too small a degree of it.

Thomas Jefferson, letter to Archibald Stewart, Dec 23, 1791

Enlightened statesmen will not always be at the helm.

James Madison, Federalist No. 10, November 23, 1787

It is one thing to be subordinate to the laws, and another to be dependent on the legislative body. The first comports

---

[60] Thaler, Richard and Sunstein, Cass. *Nudge: Improving Decisions About Health, Wealth, and Happiness.* Yale University Press. 2008. P.9

with, the last violates, the fundamental principles of good government
Alexander Hamilton, Federalist No. 71, March 18, 1788

Government, in my humble opinion, should be formed to secure and to enlarge the exercise of the natural rights of its members; and every government, which has not this in view, as its principal object, is not a government of the legitimate kind.
James Wilson, Lectures on Law, 1791

These may be but four quotes, however volumes have been written by our Founding Fathers regarding the necessity of individual liberty. They believed, as all good Americans do, that government is instituted among men to protect their freedoms not to direct or provide for their every means of sustenance.

Chapter 5
America's Legacy of Property Rights

Young man, there is America -- which at this day serves for little more than to amuse you with stories of savage men, and uncouth manners; yet shall, before you taste of death, show itself equal to the whole of that commerce which now attracts the envy of the world.

> -Edmund Burke, speech on conciliation with America, 1775[61]

It is ironic that one of England's most prominent and important leaders of the 18th Century understood America's greatness even before most of our Founding Fathers accepted the idea that we should be an independent nation. Edmund Burke saw that America's limitless potential, especially in the field of commerce would soon outstrip even the empire he loved, because Americans enjoyed the use of private property more than any people in history.

Perhaps there is no way in which America's fall from grace has been so precipitous than in the realm of private property rights. There are many things to love

---

[61] http://notable-quotes.com/b/burke_edmund.html

about America. Our Bill of Rights is a gift to humanity never before or since equaled in the entire history of civilization. However, most of the rights we cherish so deeply; free speech, freedom of religion, the right to bear arms, jury trial, etc are all but a façade covering a monolith of tyranny without our most important right: the right to private property.

Private property is how we exercise control over our lives. Nature did not provide humans with the speed, strength or agility necessary to survive, but we were bestowed with the ability to create, for our personal use, tools that shape our environment and enhance our lives. We are very fortunate that the people who carved America out of the wilderness lived in a time and place when government was often nowhere to be found and where it did exist it was relatively unobtrusive compared to the standards of today. This created an atmosphere of rugged self-reliance and most importantly entrepreneurship and gave our Founding Fathers a special appreciation for the importance of property ownership.

No discussion on private property can be said to have any meaning unless it is centered on John Locke and his *Second Treatise*. This book, written two generations before America's founding, is where some of the most important words ever written reside. I say they are the some of the most important words ever written, because Locke's philosophy, especially with regard to private property, became the bedrock of civil life in America and the intellectual justification for the Revolutionary War. Were there no *Second Treatise* there might not be an America, at least not as we know it.

Locke's discussion is built on the assertion of the original divine donation of Earth to mankind in common. He says "nobody has originally a private dominion exclusive of the rest of mankind".[62] This is very important, because it begets the argument that all men are created equal.

Locke's argument for private property can be broken down into three parts. In his own words:

1) "Tis very clear that God... has given the Earth to the children of men, given it to them in common."
2) "Though the Earth and all inferior creatures be common to all men, yet every man has property in his own person. This nobody has any right to but himself."
3) "For this labor being the unquestionable property of the laborer, no man but he can have a right to what that is once joined to, at least where there is enough and as good left in common for others."[63]

Locke's idea of a universal common should not be confused with that most evil of ideologies, Communism, in any way. Communism holds that the state owns everything, even your labor and decides how it should be used. Locke's universal common is part of man's natural state, discussed earlier, where no one owns anything except the two tools they are born with, their minds and bodies. Since our labor is an extension of both it is unquestionably our property.

Additionally, this argument assumes that nothing in nature has any value until the addition of labor. Take for example a tree bearing fruit in Locke's theoretical 'natural state'. No one owns the tree, the fruit, or the land. Although the fruit is nutritious, it does no one any good until it is picked. The act of picking the fruit is labor. Now in a person's possession through their labor the fruit is forever intertwined with that man's labor and thus is his

---

[62] Strauss, Leo and Cropsey, Joseph. *History of Political Philosophy 3rd ed.* University of Chicago press 1987. P486.
[63] Ibid p. 486-487

property. As long as the actions of the person exercising their labor, does not unduly preclude someone else from using their labor to procure fruit it can be said that fruit is rightfully the property of the person who picked it. Someone else can't take that fruit without also taking his labor, or property.

Much of the anger over British policies that caused the Revolution existed, because those policies conflicted with the obvious truths espoused by Locke. Americans were arguably the freest people in the world in 1775 when the fighting began, but that did not mean they were free. In the years between the French and Indian War and the American Revolution colonists became acutely aware of how various British policies infringed on their property rights. A few of the more important laws were:

1) The Tea Act, designed to expand the British East India Company's monopoly on the tea trade to all British Colonies to help this company out of bankruptcy. This was essentially and 18th Century version of today's bailouts. Today's Keynesian economists would have been proud of this act, but even though some historians assert it actually lowered the price of tea in the colonies, Americans hated it. It violated their property rights, because it ran counter to Locke's rule that everyone has a right to accumulate as much property as possible as long as "there is enough and as good left in common for others". Monopolies prevent others from others from using various resources for their benefit. In a land known for its obsession with entrepreneurship this is intolerable.

2) The Boston Port Act closed the port of Boston as retribution for the Tea Party, which was itself a protest of the Tea Act. The port was to be reopened when the East India Company was repaid lost revenue. By punishing an entire city for the acts of a few it violated the tenet that everything on Earth was given to man in common.

3) The Quartering Act was actually two separate acts passed in 1765 and 1774. They required colonists to

house British soldiers. By forcing families to use their homes in a way they might not wish, presupposed that the homes were the property of the crown. Since it was the colonists' labor that built their homes those dwellings were unquestionably the property of the homeowners and as Locke said "no man but he can have a right to what that is once joined to" his labor.

4) The Sugar Act was seen, in England, as a reasonable measure for defraying the cost of protecting the colonies during the war with the French. However, like the acts previously mentioned, it was passed in Parliament without allowing the colonists a voice or vote in the debates. Though it was quickly repealed the anger over 'taxation without representation' continued to simmer. It was not unlike the healthcare debates of 2009 where Americans made it crystal clear that they did not approve of the legislation, but Congress and the President passed it anyway. Unlike then, however, Americans will have a say in whether or not those politicians get to keep their jobs.

There were, of course, plenty of other acts of Parliament that enraged the colonists. Some more deserving of their ire than others, but I chose to talk about those particular acts because they directly interfered with the property rights of Americans.

APPLYING LOCKE'S PHILOSOPHY

Locke's philosophy on property rights can be found throughout the Declaration of Independence and the Constitution. In fact, it is written in to so many parts of our founding documents that I think it can be said to be the founding principle of America.

First, we should examine the Declaration of Independence. An astute observer will notice that it begins by espousing the principles of natural law and self-determination when it says:

When in the Course of human events, it becomes necessary for one people to dissolve the political bands which have connected them with another, and to assume among the powers of the earth, the separate and equal station to which the Laws of Nature and of Nature's God entitle them, a decent respect to the opinions of mankind requires that they should declare the causes which impel them to the separation.

We hold these truths to be self-evident, that all men are created equal, that they are endowed by their Creator with certain unalienable Rights, that among these are Life, Liberty and the pursuit of Happiness. That to secure these rights, Governments are instituted among Men, deriving their just powers from the consent of the governed, That whenever any Form of Government becomes destructive of these ends, it is the Right of the People to alter or to abolish it, and to institute new Government...

This may lead the reader to think these are the founding principles of the United States. However, these are not the reasons for the split with the mother country, only the justification for the actions taken. To say self-determination was the reason for the Revolution is to say America declared independence for the sake of independence. This is not true and in fact even at the time of the signing many of the Founders openly hoped for reconciliation with England. For example, on June 8th, 1776 when the resolution to draft a Declaration of Independence was proposed Edward Rutledge, an eventual signatory, noted, "no reason could be assigned for pressing into this measure, but the reason of a madman". He was joined by, among others, John Dickenson, James Wilson and Robert Livingston. They called themselves the "cool party" and considered themselves "friends of the measure", but were nonetheless reluctant to break away from England.[64]

The Declaration goes on to list 27 grievances the colonies had with the king. I will not bore you by including a long list that you can easily find and read on your own, but a large plurality of the offenses deal directly or indirectly with the property rights of the colonists. Five deal with taxation without representation, four assert the violation of property rights through bureaucracy, denial of trade and outright theft, two deal with the quartering of large standing armies and one charges the king with theft of individuals' labor through the impressments of sailors. Of course, not all the grievances deal with property rights. Most of the others are concerned mainly with corruption in the legal system, but even that influences the exercising of property rights.

The Constitution is similarly concerned with protecting our property rights. For example, Article 1 Section 9 lists the limits on Congress' power. Though not all concern property rights, about half do. They include prohibitions on bills of attainder and ex post facto laws which violate the principles of no taxation without representation it also provided that "no capitation, or other direct, tax shall be laid, unless in proportion to the census enumeration herein before directed to be taken" which was a fancy 18th Century way of prohibiting an income tax. Sadly that part of the Constitution was superseded by the 16th Amendment. Article 1 Section 9 also forbids Congress from passing any tax or duty on articles exported from any state or giving preference to the ports of any one state over another.

The restrictions placed on the federal government by Article 1 Section 9 are important because they underscore the private nature of property ownership. If Congress were allowed to lay taxes on exports or favor

---

[64] McCullough, David. *John Adams*. New York 2001. P.118.

one port over another it would have to first presume that the federal government had a right to that property. The same can be said about income taxes. Taxes on income are really nothing more than taxes on an individual's labor. Remember, central to Locke's thesis on property rights was that "for this labor being the unquestionable property of the laborer, no man but he can have a right to what that is once joined to". Income taxes are nothing more than the government forcibly taking a portion of an individual's property; also known as theft. Another, less rosy, way of looking at it is the government stealing a portion of an individual's labor; also known as slavery.

The 16th Amendment may have made this form of theft and slavery legal, but it is in no way right. It is the first step in what the Founders feared most about democracy; that one group would grow powerful enough to literally steal from another group with the full support of the United States government.

GOVERNMENT AS A SAFE GUARD OF PROPERTY RIGHTS

As we have seen, the property rights of individuals were never very far from the minds of the Founding Fathers. In fact they envisioned the Federal Government as a bulwark for the defense of just that. Hamilton, always the pragmatist, argued in favor of the Constitution partly because he believed it would limit the cost of government and help keep taxes low. Writing as Publius he said:

The money saved from one object may be usefully applied to another, and there will be so much the less to be drawn from the pockets of the people. If the States are united under one government, there will be but one national civil list to support; if they are divided into several confederacies, there will be as many different national civil lists to be provided for--and each of them, as to the principal departments, coextensive with that which would be necessary for a government of the whole.[65]

Clearly, with federal spending close to $4 trillion a year, we have strayed from this vision. The Founding Fathers understood that government is generally a drain on the economy. A recent study by the Harvard Business School backs up the timeless wisdom of the Founders. It found that increased government spending actually hurts economies in the long term. The authors found:

Statistically and economically significant evidence that firms respond to government spending shocks by: 1) reducing investments in new capital, 2) reducing investments in R&D, and 3) paying out more to shareholders in the face of this reduced investment opportunity set. Further, we find that when the spending shocks reverse (through a relinquishing of chairmanship), most all of these behaviors reverse. Finally, we also find some evidence that firms scale back their employment, and experience a decline in sales growth.[66]

Another damning indictment of federal spending is the current national unemployment rate. According to the Bureau of Labor Statistics the unemployment rate in January 2009, When Barrack Obama took office was 8.1%. In October 2010, more than a year after he and the Democratic controlled Congress passed the largest government-spending bill in history, the unemployment rate was 10.4%[67] The Harvard study and BLS unemployment estimates make painfully clear what

---

[65] Hamilton, Federalist 13.

[66] Choen, Lauren et al. *Do Powerful Politicians Cause Corporate Downsizing?* Harvard Business School and NBER. March 16, 2010
http://www.people.hbs.edu/cmalloy/pdffiles/envaloy.pdf
[67]
http://data.bls.gov:8080/PDQ/servlet/SurveyOutputServlet;jsessionid=6230c52a9e5645316664

common sense should already tell us, that populist rhetoric and rampant government spending always damage the economy. Of course we could have avoided so much of our current economic pain if we had simply followed the advice of those who came before us. After his famous travels through America, Alexis De Tocqueville noted:

Democracy attaches all possible value to each man… while socialism makes each man a mere agent, a mere number. Democracy and socialism have nothing in common but one word: equality. But notice the difference: while democracy seeks equality in liberty, socialism seeks equality in restraint and servitude.[68]

However, even in the years immediately after America fought a bloody war to reduce the scope of government, there was significant debate over how government should spend. One of the most pressing issues after the Revolution was the war debt. At the time each state amassed individual debts along with the Continental Congress.

Hamilton was probably the most vocal advocate for an active government. He wanted the federal government to assume the war debt for every state. His motives were more nationalist than economic. He believed doing so would bind the new states together and safe guard against insurrection. Madison on the other hand feared such a move would disenfranchise the original bondholders, especially war widows and veterans while enriching speculators. As it turns out both men were right. Hamilton got his way and the states were bound more tightly as a result. Unfortunately the average, often poor, citizens received only pennies on the dollar for their bonds

---

[68] Quoted in [68] Levin, Mark. *Liberty and Tyranny.* Simon and Schuster. 2009 p.91

while the speculators who purchased them a few years earlier were paid at par.[69]

A similar scenario played out after President Obama signed into law his bailouts of the auto industry. The original bondholders of GM, the people who risked capital to help the company grow, would have been the first in line to receive payment had the company been allowed to go into bankruptcy as law and tradition require. However, the government's takeover, and subsequent restructuring, of the auto maker instead gave a greater stake in the company to government regulators and union bosses, while leaving bondholders and common stockholders to take millions of dollars of losses in what should have been relatively safe investments. Many of these bondholders were far from the rich the Left loves to hate. They also included pension funds for teachers and civil servants and 401(k) owners like you and me.

---

[69] Bennett, William J. America: The Last Best Hope. Nashville, TN. 2007. P.145

Chapter 6
The Judiciary

If outrage over the curtailment of property rights was the driving force behind our split with Britain, then corruption in the judiciary was a very close second. Jefferson listed in the Declaration of Independence at least eight grievances the colonists had with King George in this regard. Most of their grievances dealt with the colonists' inability to receive a fair trial. It was common practice at the time for individuals to be denied jury trial or to be arrested and sent to England for trails where the outcome was already predetermined. These problems have been almost entirely rectified today as we enjoy one of the most open and free legal systems in the world. However, a few problems the colonists had continue to stifle liberty in America to this day. Unfortunately it is not from a foreign power, but of our own doing.

The relevant lines of the Declaration read:

He has made judges dependent on his will alone, for the tenure of their offices, and the amount and payment of their salaries.

He has erected a multitude of new offices, and sent hither swarms of officers to harass our people, and eat out their substance.

He has combined with others to subject us to a jurisdiction foreign to our constitution, and unacknowledged by our laws; giving his assent to their acts of pretended legislation

Today, the judiciary is still used to override the will of the people. Every year we see dozens of ballot initiatives or legitimate acts of legislature overturned by a small handful of judges. Few people are as familiar with this as the citizens of California. In 2008 the California Supreme Court overturned a 2000 ballot initiative called the Defense of Marriage Act. With this ruling "four judges discarded the votes of 4,618,673 Californians" and essentially imposed a new law on the people of California without their consent.[70]

2008 was by no means the first time this happened either. In 1994 Californians passed by a margin of 59% to 41% proposition 187, which limited education, healthcare and social services to illegal aliens. Even with the obvious support of the people, the law was declared unconstitutional and never enforced.[71]

That seems reasonable enough. If people are in this country illegally, they are already criminals. We should not compound the problem by giving them billions of dollars in free services. In both cases the people of California made their voices clear, but were over ridden by as few as four people. Such atrocious judicial overreach amounts to oligarchy.

Today the results are clear. California was once envy of the world in every regard. Today the state is utterly bankrupt, its hospitals are closing at alarming rates and its prisons are overflowing with the citizens of other countries.

We have today a judiciary that stands in judgment not just of the other two branches of government, but also

---

[70] *CA Supreme Court Imposes Same-Sex 'Marriage,' Overturning Prop. 22.* Reuters May 15, 2008. http://www.reuters.com/article/idUS240582+15-May-2008+PRN20080515

[71] *California Ballot Measure Targets Illegal Immigrants.* July, 16 2009. http://www.npr.org/templates/story/story.php?storyId=106657563

of the people. Its word is final and injustice on the part of the judiciary can only be redressed by a constitutional amendment, which is extremely difficult to attain, or by waiting for judges to retire and be replaced, which can take decades. Amazingly, this may be the one problem our Founding Fathers were not far sighted enough to foresee. They truly believed the judiciary would be impartial and the weakest branch of government.

Writing in Federalist 78, Alexander Hamilton explained that because only the legislature will make the laws and only the executive can enforce them the courts will have neither "force nor will, but merely judgment" behind their decision. He goes further and says:

This simple view of the matter suggests several important consequences... It equally proves, that though individual oppression may now and then proceed from the courts of justice, the general liberty of the people can never be endangered from that quarter.[72]

Given this point of view, Hamilton would probably respond to me, by saying that I simply listed a couple of court decisions with which I disagreed and though they may have been constitutionally unsound decisions they do not show an inherent flaw in the legal process or persecution of a particular group.

Though, I could never match wits with Alexander Hamilton I think the persecution of one group in particular by the courts would prove my point. That group is Christians. Let's begin by looking at how the legal system has been turned against adherents of the Christian faith.

For more than thirty years the courts have been inundated with various law suits by groups like the ACLU designed to prevent Christians from publicly exercising their faith. Consider the recent example of *Christian Legal*

---

[72] Alexander Hamilton, Federalist 78

Society v. Martinez. In the June 28, 2010 decision the Supreme Court held that a college could refuse to recognize a Christian club based on the fact that it requires its members to adhere to tenets of the Christian faith, specifically a ban on homosexual activity.[73] This decision stands in stark contrast to a 2006 decision where the court upheld that the federal government could withhold funds to public universities unless they allow military recruiters on campus.[74]

Though I agree with the Court's unanimous decision to allow recruiters on campus it cannot be denied that the military excludes people for all manner of differences, be they age, gender, disability and (as of the date of the 2006 ruling in Rumsfeld v. FAIR) sexual orientation. Why would the court rule that it is proper for the government to exclude individuals based on sexual orientation, but private religious groups cannot? This glaring inconsistency is a clear violation of the individual Christian Legal Society members' right of association.

It is all too common for Christians and Christian symbols to be singled out by the court system as unconstitutional even when other religious groups act in exactly the same way at the same time. Take for example the 1989 case of *County of Allegheny v. ACLU*. In this case the American Civil Liberties Union sued to have a nativity scene removed from the Allegheny courthouse steps, because they viewed it as an unconstitutional endorsement of religion. However, they were unconcerned with the 18-foot menorah also displayed on the courthouse property. Sadly, in a split 5 to 4 decision the Supreme Court ruled in the ACLU's favor.[75]

The logic defying reasoning presented by the court was that since the menorah was situated next to a

---

[73] Supreme Court Ruling in *Christian Legal Society V. Martinez*. June 28, 2010 http://www.supremecourt.gov/opinions/09pdf/08-1371.pdf

[74] Supreme Court Ruling in Rumsfeld V. FAIR. March 6, 2006.

[75] *County of Allegheny v. ACLU*, 492 U.S. 573 (1989)

Christmas tree it represented a celebration of diversity instead of religion, while the nativity scene stood alone. There are two major problems with this flawed line of reasoning. First and foremost all three objects appeared together as part of the courthouse decorations and remained up for the same period of time. Secondly, a Christmas tree is a secular, not religious, symbol therefore the menorah was also standing alone as a religious symbol.

Today the courts have become such a powerful instrument in removing Christianity from the public square that even the threat of litigation can change traditions held for years. In 2004 the ACLU succeeded in having a small cross removed from the seal of Los Angeles through their usual tactics of intimidation while at the same time a Federal court ruled that seventh graders could be forced to recite Muslim prayers in school.[76]

Legal objections to all things Christian are nothing new for California. It took sixteen years of legal thugery, but eventually the city of San Diego was forced to remove a 43-foot cross, located for more than 50 years, at a veterans' memorial. James McElroy, the attorney who sued to have the cross removed argued, the cross was there illegally, because "it's a preeminent Christian symbol on public land. It's a pretty simple call".[77] Of course, this argument is patently ridiculous when one considers the multitude of Christian symbols on the graves of soldiers buried at Arlington Cemetery. There on our nation's most sacred land, symbols from many religions abound, but none so much as the cross.

It is only fair to point out that in all of these cases, the justices did not actively seek to persecute Christians. The cases were brought before them and whether we agree or disagree with their rulings they did have to rule.

---

[76] http://www.foxnews.com/story/0,2933,124012,00.html

[77] http://www.washingtonpost.com/wp-dyn/articles/A21598-2005Mar9.html

However, a very disturbing trend is developing. In all of these cases Christians were barred from openly expressing their religious views by the declarations of five or fewer individuals, because they felt doing so would offend others. The court system has been so badly corrupted that freedom of thought is now at risk if anyone deems that thought offensive.

HOW DID IT COME TO THIS?

The Founding Fathers absolutely wanted an independent judiciary that could void laws created by the legislature if those laws conflicted with the Constitution, but their vision was of a judiciary that used only the narrowest possible interpretation of the Constitution and ONLY the Constitution in making the decisions. Hamilton explains in Federalist 78:

Nor does this conclusion by any means suppose a superiority of the judicial to the legislative power. It only supposes that the power of the people is superior to both; and that where the will of the legislature, declared in its statutes, stands in opposition to that of the people, declared in the Constitution, the judges ought to be governed by the latter rather than the former. They ought to regulate their decisions by the fundamental laws, rather than by those which are not fundamental.[78]

Here, Hamilton gave us an unambiguous strict constructionist doctrine of legal interpretation. Indeed, that is the only way we can survive as a nation of laws and not of men. Unfortunately, many of the most powerful judges today openly flaunt and dispute this bedrock of American jurisprudence. Many force foreign law upon Americans. Ruth Bader Ginsberg, for example has said "Why

---

[78] Hamilton, Alexander. Federalist 78

shouldn't we look to the wisdom of a judge from abroad with at least as much ease as we would read a law review article written by a professor?"[79]

Well, Justice Ginsberg, there are a few very good reasons why. Government officials take an oath to defend *The Constitution of the United States* not the laws of whichever foreign nation they like the most. Americans are only capable of exerting control over American lawmakers and as such can only consent to be held responsible for adhering to American laws. Using foreign law to decide cases in American courts amounts to the statutory rape of the American legal system.

There is another grave problem with her logic. Which laws, from which countries should be used? The laws in Germany are far different from the laws in Saudi Arabia. Who is to say which is correct? Well, it is the American people who are to say which is correct. They decide the merits of the laws through their elected representatives, ballot initiatives and constitutional amendments. The point is using foreign law is nothing more than a thinly veiled excuse for a judge to rule based on personal preference rather than the constitutionally sanctioned laws passed by our duly elected officials.

The origins of her and so many other judges' troubling interpretation of the law can be traced back to what I believe is a fundamental misinterpretation the most consequential court case in American history, Marbury V. Madison.

We all learned in high school that Marbury V. Madison established the principle of judicial review and established the Supreme Court as the final arbiter of a law's constitutionality. This interpretation hangs on the phrase "It is emphatically the province and duty of the

---

[79] *Ginsburg Shares Views on Influence of Foreign Law on Her Court, and Vice Versa.* NY Times, April 11, 2009
http://www.nytimes.com/2009/04/12/us/12ginsburg.html

judicial department to say what the law is".[80] That seems pretty cut and dry. Those seventeen words have been used as the basis for all judicial activism for more than 200 years, but they are only seventeen words from a document of more than *ten thousand*. If I were to include the full text of that document formatted in the same way this book is formatted, it would take up nearly 50 pages. And we use just 17 words to establish all legal precedent! That is nonsense. If one were to further read the ruling one would find this interesting passage:

By the constitution of the United States, the president is invested with certain important political powers, in the [5 U.S. 137, 166] exercise of which he is to use his own discretion, and is accountable only to his country in his political character, and to his own conscience. To aid him in the performance of these duties, he is authorized to appoint certain officers, who act by his authority and in conformity with his orders.

In such cases, their acts are his acts; and whatever opinion may be entertained of the manner in which executive discretion may be used, still there exists, and can exist, no power to control that discretion.[81]

Here we see that even though Marbury V. Madison established the Supreme Court as the final word in most cases, it also limits it in others. If the Constitution grants a specific power to the President, only the people have a right to judge the way he uses that power. Logic dictates that this rule must be applied equally to all branches and levels of government, thus only the people and not the Supreme Court can be the final arbiter of what is and is not constitutional.

---

[80] Supreme Court Ruling in *Marbury V. Madison*. Feb 1803.
http://caselaw.lp.findlaw.com/scripts/getcase.pl?navby=case&court=us&vol=5&page=137
[81] Ibid

And what would Chief Justice Marshall think of Ginsberg and her use of foreign law in deciding cases? Almost immediately after writing "It is emphatically the province and duty of the judicial department to say what the law is" he goes on to write:

Those then who controvert the principle that the constitution is to be considered, in court, as a paramount law, are reduced to the necessity of maintaining that courts must close their eyes on the constitution, and see only the law. This doctrine would subvert the very foundation of all written constitutions. It would declare that an act, which, according to the principles and theory of our government, is entirely void, is yet, in practice, completely obligatory. It would declare, that if the legislature shall do what is expressly forbidden, such act, notwithstanding the express prohibition, is in reality effectual. It would be giving to the legislature a practical and real omnipotence with the same breath, which professes to restrict their powers within narrow limits. It is prescribing limits, and declaring that those limits may be passed at pleasure.[82]

Apparently he would be appalled with her judicial philosophy.

---

[82] Ibid

Chapter 7
Foreign Policy

It may surprise most people to learn that America's struggle with Islamic terrorism is nothing new. If asked when it began some might say with the fall of the Shah of Iran and the hostage crisis that ensued or with the bombing of Marine barracks in Lebanon. They would be wrong. In fact it dates back to before the founding of America.

From the 16th to 19th century, the Barbary Pirates plagued the Mediterranean Sea. These unscrupulous terrorists would capture merchant vessels and raid the coastal cities of Spain, France, Italy and even from time to time as far north as England looking to kidnap victims for their slave trade. Between 1530 and 1780 as many as 1.25 million Europeans and Americans were taken as slaves.[83]

In 1785 when then Ambassadors Thomas Jefferson and John Adams met with Tripoli's envoy to London, Ambassador Sidi Haji Abdrahaman they asked him what gave his country the right to enslave innocent people. Jefferson later transmitted the answer he received

---

[83] Davis, Robert. Christian Slaves, Muslim Masters: White Slavery in the Mediterranean, The Barbary Coast, and Italy, 1500-1800. Macmillan Publishers Limited 2010. P. 23

to John Jay, who was then the Secretary of Foreign Affairs:

> *It was written in their Qu'ran, that all nations which had not acknowledged the Prophet were sinners, whom it was the right and duty of the faithful to plunder and enslave; and that every Muslim who was slain in this warfare was sure to go to paradise.*[84]

Sound familiar? I am not brining up this point to establish some sort of moral high ground, because obviously during the same period Europeans and Americans engaged in their own slave trades. To say one was worse than another would be a digression into irrelevancy and well beyond the scope of this book. However, the analogies between America's Barbary conflicts of the early 19th Century and our current War on Terrorism are strong enough to teach us a few lessons on how to solve some of today's problems.

TERRORISM IN THE 19TH CENTURY

It is clear from Jefferson's dealing with Tripoli's Ambassador that little changed in the islamo-facist mindset between 1785 and September 11, 2001. Just as we are dealing with Muslim extremists who use their religion to justify killing innocents, so did our country's first leaders. The major difference was they did not have the luxury of commanding the world's most powerful military. In fact when we finally confronted the problem, we had almost no military to speak of.

The problem continued for years after Jefferson's encounter with Ambassador Abdrahaman. By the time

---

[84] Letter from Thomas Jefferson to John Jay," March 28, 1786, "Thomas Jefferson Papers," Series 1. General Correspondence. 1651-1827, Library of Congress. LoC: March 28, 1786.

Jefferson ascended to the presidency, he and America were ready to fight back. The only question was how?

When Jefferson assumed the presidency in 1801 he was greeted with a demand for tribute from Tripoli, a common practice used to prevent the Barbary Pirates from taking more slaves. Jefferson was fed up with the constant cycle of extortion and refused. This prompted a declaration of war against America from Tripoli. America quickly cobbled together a fleet and took the fight directly to the terrorists.

Jefferson's war effort was plagued by some of the same problems as our modern war on terrorism from the beginning. America was limited in its options by a complete lack of overseas bases, much in the same way the war efforts in Afghanistan and Iraq were initially hampered over basing and over flight rights in Pakistan, Turkey and Saudi Arabia. There was also an effort to conduct the war on the cheap and without an actual declaration of war. Sound familiar?

Jefferson, however, had a couple good excuses. This was America's first expeditionary war effort. No one knew exactly how to even get started. America was also without an army or navy of any consequence. These things had to be created hastily.

Despite initial missteps, Jefferson's war was punctuated by brilliant acts of heroism and daring by men like Stephen Decatur, whose midnight raid to destroy a captured American warship was called "the most bold and daring act of the age" by famed British Admiral Horatio Nelson.[85] It also resulted in the very first instance the Stars and Stripes were hoisted above foreign soil in victory.

On June 4, 1805 America was able to negotiate a treaty that provided for the release of all Americans and American property wrongfully held by the Bashaw of

---

[85] Tucker, Spencer. *Stephen Decatur: a life most bold and daring*. Naval Institue. 2005. P.ix

Tripoli. Unfortunately it also required America to pay $60,000 ransom for the release of the prisoners. This combined with America's growing tensions with Great Britain caused the peace to last only two years. By the end of 1807 Americans once again risked enslavement when they crossed through the Straights of Gibraltar. Though America gained prestige and experience that would prove invaluable in 1812, it was essentially in the same position as it began.

The War of 1812 emboldened America in foreign affairs. Less than a week after the signing of the Treaty of Ghent, President Madison asked Congress for a declaration of war to end the raids by the Barbary pirates on American commercial shipping once and for all.[86] In March 1815, Captain Stephen Decatur returned to the Barbary Coast with a fleet of ten ships. They captured two Algerian gunboats and threatened to bombard the city. As a result of this overwhelming show of military resolve, the North African states agreed to treaties releasing American prisoners without ransom, ending all demands for American tribute, and providing compensation for American vessels that had been seized.[87]

America's first anti-terror effort is very instructive for our current struggle. First and foremost, just because we have declared victory in Iraq and it appears some negotiated settlement may be possible in Afghanistan, does not mean we won yet. The moment we turn our attention away from these efforts we could end up where we were on Sept. 10, 2001. Constant vigilance is the first priority in fending off Islamic terror.

Second, we can't assume we can do these wars on the cheap. Committing to military action necessitates the overwhelming use of force to end the conflict quickly and

[86] Whipple, ABC. *To the shores of Tripoli: the birth of the U.S. Navy and Marines*. Naval Institute. 1991. P.276

[87] Mintz, S. (2007). *Digital History*. Retrieved (1 November 2010) from http://www.digitalhistory.uh.edu/database/article_display.cfm?HHID=573

on our terms. Jefferson's effort lasted almost four years, because America jumped hastily into the war and tried to do it as inexpensively as possible. Madison's effort, by contrast, took only months to secure a lasting and unconditional victory, because America applied the maximum amount of force it was capable of from the very beginning.

THE COMPETING VISIONS

Over the course of the 20th Century, Americans were thrust into some extraordinary circumstances. Their heroism in both world wars, generosity in rebuilding the world afterwards and courage in facing the Soviet Union not only saved billions of people from tyranny, but also set up America as the preeminent world power. We should all be proud of our country's place in the world. America is a beacon for freedom and when she is successful everyone in the world can benefit, but is our current superpower status really what the Founding Fathers wanted? Did they break from England in order to create an equally dominant empire? In most cases their motives and visions were actually just the opposite.

The Founding Fathers clearly wanted a foreign policy strong enough to dissuade America's rivals from attacking her and able to protect her economic interests overseas. Writing as Publius in Federalist #4, John Jay opined "We have heard much of the fleets of Britain, and the time may come, if we are wise, when the fleets of America may engage attention."

Alexander Hamilton probably had the most ambitious plans for the new nation. He advocated having the Federal Government assume the war debts of the states, creating a national bank and using protective trade practices like tariffs and other import duties to create the foundation for the industrialization of America. With this incredibly ambitious vision Hamilton wanted to bring

America into direct economic competition with England, especially with regard to industry.

Jefferson, on the other hand, opposed Hamilton's plans. His vision was of a quiet, agrarian nation. Jefferson believed that by shunning industrial growth and embracing agrarian lifestyles America would best keep to its republican principles.[88]

Though this important debate between Hamilton and Jefferson may seem economic in nature it was in many ways a foreign policy struggle. In the short term Jefferson's vision prevailed, but as America's status as the largest economy in the world can attest it was Hamilton's vision that endured. Maintaining the world's largest economy also requires a massive navy and merchant marine force and accessible ports throughout the world. It requires extensive treaties and political ties with other nations.

All of this brings America into direct competition with other nations necessitating an even more aggressive foreign policy, which of course exposes America to greater risk from abroad. By contrast Jefferson's view would not have brought great wealth to America but it would not require nearly as much of the things previously mentioned. It is logical to conclude that Jefferson's vision would have required a much less energetic foreign policy.

ADAMS AND A NATION DIVIDED

John Adams is in my opinion one of the most underrated presidents. A 2009 C-Span survey of 64 historians ranked Adams 19th out of 43 (President Obama was not included in the survey).[89] Sure he made the top 50%, but only just barely. I'd easily put him in the top 10.

---

[88] Mintz, S. (2007). *Digital History*. Retrieved (1 November 2010) from http://www.digitalhistory.uh.edu/database/article_display.cfm?HHID=6
[89] http://www.c-span.org/PresidentialSurvey/Overall-Ranking.aspx

Adams' reputation probably suffers from two unfortunate measures of presidential effectiveness: reelection and personal likeability. These are arbitrary metrics that really only examine how people felt about presidential actions, not their lasting effects.

Adams' major contribution to American foreign policy came as a result from what has come to be known as the Quasi-War with France. Almost, from the very beginning of Washington's presidency the country was divided into two foreign policy camps. The Federalists, led by Alexander Hamilton favored stronger ties with England. The Anti-Federalists (also known by the somewhat confusing moniker of Democratic-Republicans) were enchanted by the French culture and the French revolution.

In 1795 Washington submitted the *Treaty of Amity Commerce and Navigation, between His Britannic Majesty; and The United States of America*, commonly known as Jay's Treaty, to the Senate for ratification. It was a rather unpopular piece of legislation. Hamilton's camp believed it did not go far enough in securing commercial relations with England and Jefferson's camp thought it went too far and alienated our former allies, the French. For Washington's part, he was lukewarm to it. He also believed that it was not the best possible deal for America, but understood that we were not negotiating from a position of strength. In July 1795 he wrote to Secretary of State Edmund Randolph:

My opinion respecting the treaty, is the same now that it was: namely, not favorable to it, but that it is better to ratify it in the manner the Senate have advised (and with the reservation already mentioned), than to suffer matters to remain as they are, unsettled.[90]

---

[90] http://www.loc.gov/rr/program/bib/ourdocs/jay.html

It was an imperfect treaty, but it kept us out of war with England. Unfortunately, by the time John Adam's assumed the presidency we now faced war with an irate France, that had begun attacking and seizing American merchant ships.

As the first Federalist president, Adams' political base expected him to embrace war with France. However, Vice President Thomas Jefferson led a vocal and influential push to avoid war at all cost with his beloved France. Adams wanted no part of war, but as president could not stand by and allow American merchants to suffer at the hands of French privateers.

His solution was to prepare for war by building anew the US Navy while continuing to sue for peace. Rather than declare all out war, Adams sought a middle ground and received authority from Congress to attack French vessels on the high seas, but contained most naval action to the Caribbean.[91] A peace treaty was ratified by both nations on December 21, 1801. America was able to show resolve to the international community and negotiate a mutually beneficial peace with France, but Adam's political career was over.

Adams' refusal to give in to the radical forces of both sides kept America out of a larger and more destructive war, while bringing a relatively quick end to what could have been a devastatingly nebulous conflict. However, his stance left him with few friends in Washington DC and in 1800 he lost his reelection bid to the infinitely more charismatic Thomas Jefferson. For taking a principled stance that he knew would ruin his political career, but was best for the country John Adams displayed moral courage that we seldom see from politicians in any era.

---

[91] Act Further to Protect the Commerce of the United States. July 9, 1798.   , http://memory.loc.gov/cgi-bin/ampage?collId=llsl&fileName=001/llsl001.db&recNum=701

THE MADISON VIEW

When examining the wisdom of the Founding Fathers it is important to not just look at what they believed, but why they held their beliefs. The subject of a standing military is a prime example. With the possible exception of Alexander Hamilton, the Founders were nearly unanimous in the belief that a standing army is one of the greatest threats to a republic. However, they also understood that a successful nation must be able to project its power at any time. I believe this is why the Army and Navy are sanctioned separately in the Constitution.

The conventional wisdom is they feared standing armies, because of the temptation to use them to raid citizens' homes in the middle of the night and violently oppress minority groups. This was to some degree their experience under the British, but our fighting men and women have proved over the last century that fear is no longer valid. Indeed, the US military has proven to be not only the muscle of the United States, but also its moral backbone. Even so there is a nugget of truth in their view on standing armies that is still relevant. Consider this quote from James Madison on war:

Of all the enemies to public liberty war is, perhaps, the most to be dreaded, because it comprises and develops the germ of every other. War is the parent of armies; from these proceed debts and taxes; and armies, and debts, and taxes are the known instruments for bringing the many under the domination of the few. In war, too, the discretionary power of the Executive is extended; its influence in dealing out offices, honors, and emoluments is multiplied; and all the means of seducing the minds, are added to those of subduing the force, of the people. The same malignant aspect in republicanism may be traced in the inequality of fortunes, and the opportunities of fraud, growing out of a state of war, and in the degeneracy of manners and of morals engendered by both. No nation could preserve its freedom in the midst of continual warfare.[92]

If you look this quote up on the internet you will be inundated with ultra-liberal websites. In fact you will be hard pressed to find a legitimate source for this quote. As you would expect, they use it to vilify America, George W Bush and the War on Terror. Also, just as you would expect, they completely miss the point.

Carefully reread the passage. He is not demonizing America's use of force or the military. In fact he was the first president to ask Congress for a declaration war. Instead he is warning us about the dangers of corruption, debt, taxation and civil unrest inherent in a permanent war footing. Indeed we have seen all of this in America's two longest wars, Vietnam and the War on Terror.

All Madison is saying is that we must carefully analyze any use of force to ensure that it will end as quickly as possible and keep our national security apparatus postured in such a way as to simultaneously deter enemy aggression and deter our own impulses toward military adventurism. In other words, we would be wise to keep our military home as much as possible and avoid being the world police.

WASHINGTON AND NEUTRALITY

George Washington probably gave us the most important vision for our foreign policy. The most famous example of this is his farewell address where he said:

The great rule of conduct for us in regard to foreign nations is in extending our commercial relations, to have with them as little political connection as possible.

---

[92] *Letters and Other Writings of James Madison* (1865), Vol. IV, p. 491

So far as we have already formed engagements, let them be fulfilled with perfect good faith. Here let us stop. Europe has a set of primary interests, which to us have none; or a very remote relation. Hence she must be engaged in frequent controversies, the causes of which are essentially foreign to our concerns. Hence, therefore, it must be unwise in us to implicate ourselves by artificial ties in the ordinary vicissitudes of her politics, or the ordinary combinations and collisions of her friendships or enmities.[93]

Contrary to what we are often taught he does not outright decry alliances with other nations. Actually, he emphatically states that we must fulfill our treaty obligations. What he does wish, however, is that we generally confine our foreign intercourse to commercial relations as much as possible. He and many of his contemporaries were terrified that strong political attachments would drag America into the senseless wars of Europe. Just prior to the passage above Washington wrote:

Against the insidious wiles of foreign influence (I conjure you to believe me, fellow-citizens) the jealousy of a free people ought to be constantly awake, since history and experience prove that foreign influence is one of the most baneful foes of republican government. But that jealousy to be useful must be impartial; else it becomes the instrument of the very influence to be avoided, instead of a defense against it. Excessive partiality for one foreign nation and excessive dislike of another cause those whom they actuate to see danger only on one side, and serve to veil and even second the arts of influence on the other. Real patriots who may resist the intrigues of the favorite are liable to become suspected and odious, while its tools

---

[93] George Washington's Farewell Address. September 19, 1796.

and dupes usurp the applause and confidence of the
people, to surrender their interests.[94]

Obviously we live in a very different world today. Our vast oceans are no longer enough to protect us from foreign-born violence and our vast economy reaches every corner of the world, necessitating a powerful military to protect our national interests. Still one must wonder if Washington would think we were committing national suicide by becoming so deeply involved with Middle East nations while steadfastly refusing to tap our own vast fossil fuel resources.

The Founders' point of view was from that of a nation barely able to defend itself in a world dominated by giants. Today America is that giant, but would they still approve of permanent military alliances like NATO or our enduring presence in the nations of South Korea, Japan, Germany, England, Italy, Turkey, Spain, Iraq, Oman, Afghanistan, Saudi Arabia, Kuwait, Bahrain and Qatar?

---

[94] Ibid

Chapter 8
The Proper Role of Government

Justice is the end of government. It is the end of civil society.
-Federalist 51

Ultimately every question we have endeavored to answer in this book has led to this one. What is the role of government? It is a question man has been trying to answer since the beginning of civil society and no one has ever gotten it completely correct. As flawed creatures we are incapable of completely divorcing our prejudices and desires from our intellect and reason. Fortunately, in forging a new nation our Founding Fathers were wise enough to avoid elevating any one man's view above another without careful deliberation.

The Founders set forth a blueprint of government where in many respects the national government is intended to be weaker than the state and local governments. However, just as with religion, the Founding Fathers were not always of one mind as to the role of government. Despite their differences they created an amazing document that balanced all interests.

The Constitution is the supreme law of the land. As such it should be interpreted literally and in the narrowest sense possible. Indeed, that is the way the father of the Constitution believed it should be interpreted. On January 10, 1794 while debating in the House of Representatives over a bill to offer financial support to refugees in St. Domingo James Madison was recorded saying:

> *The government of the United States is a definite government, confined to specified objects. It is not like the state governments, whose powers are more general. Charity is no part of the legislative duty of the government. It would puzzle any gentleman to lay his finger on any part of the Constitution which would authorize the government to interpose in the relief of the St. Domingo sufferers.*[95]

Can you imagine a politician today taking such a position, which could so easily be twisted, in order to defend the highest ideals of our country? There can be no doubt our Founding Fathers did NOT want our Constitution to be a 'living document'. With that in mind we will now endeavor to examine what limits and responsibilities it gives the various portions of government.

THE LEGISLATURE

Article 1 Section 8 of the Constitution lays out the powers delegated to Congress. We know from our previous discussions that the Founding Fathers intended the Federal Government to act only when it is specifically authorized to do so. By taking a look at just what Congress is authorized to do we can see how truly bloated

---

[95] Elliot's Debates, vol 4. http://memory.loc.gov/cgi-bin/query/r?ammem/hlaw:@field(DOCID+@lit(ed00423)):

our government has become. The only things Congress is authorized to do under the Constitution are:

- *To lay and collect taxes, duties, imposts and excises, to pay the debts and provide for the common defense and general welfare of the United States; but all duties, imposts and excises shall be uniform throughout the United States*
- *To borrow money on the credit of the United States*
- *To regulate Commerce with foreign Nations, and among the several States, and with the Indian Tribes*
- *To establish an uniform Rule of Naturalization, and uniform Laws on the subject of Bankruptcies throughout the United States*
- *To coin Money, regulate the Value thereof, and of foreign Coin, and fix the Standard of Weights and Measures*
- *To provide for the Punishment of counterfeiting the Securities and current Coin of the United States*
- *To establish Post Offices and Post Roads*
- *To promote the Progress of Science and useful Arts, by securing for limited Times to Authors and Inventors the exclusive Right to their respective Writings and Discoveries*
- *To constitute Tribunals inferior to the Supreme Court*
- *To define and punish Piracies and Felonies committed on the high Seas, and Offenses against the Law of Nations*
- *To declare War, grant Letters of Marque and Reprisal, and make Rules concerning Captures on Land and Water*
- *To raise and support Armies, but no Appropriation of Money to that Use shall be for a longer Term than two Years*
- *To provide and maintain a Navy*
- *To make Rules for the Government and Regulation of the land and naval Forces*

- *To provide for calling forth the Militia to execute the Laws of the Union, suppress Insurrections and repel Invasions*
- *To provide for organizing, arming, and disciplining, the Militia, and for governing such Part of them as may be employed in the Service of the United States, reserving to the States respectively, the Appointment of the Officers, and the Authority of training the Militia according to the discipline prescribed by Congress*
- *To exercise exclusive Legislation in all Cases whatsoever, over such District (not exceeding ten Miles square) as may, by Cession of particular States, and the acceptance of Congress, become the Seat of the Government of the United States, and to exercise like Authority over all Places purchased by the Consent of the Legislature of the State in which the Same shall be, for the Erection of Forts, Magazines, Arsenals, dock-Yards, and other needful Buildings*
- *To make all Laws which shall be necessary and proper for carrying into Execution the foregoing Powers, and all other Powers vested by this Constitution in the Government of the United States, or in any Department or Officer thereof.*

Clearly Article 1 Section 8 does not authorize Social Security, Medicare, Obamacare, welfare, the Department of Education, the Department of Energy, the National Endowment of the Arts, TARP, corporate bailouts and trillions of dollars worth of other federal programs. When one considers Article 1 Section 8 in conjunction with the 10th Amendment it becomes clear that all of these and a myriad of others are unconstitutional. That is not to say they can't be operated constitutionally. It just has to be at the state level.

THE STATES

The 10th Amendment of the Bill of Rights states:

The powers not delegated to the United States by the Constitution, nor prohibited by it to the States, are reserved to the States respectively, or to the people.

This amendment is easily the most overlooked, mostly because progressives were so successful in pushing national level policies during the 20th Century. The irony is that it authorizes just about any hair brained, liberal scheme at the state level. The reason progressives were so voracious in pushing big government programs at the national as opposed to the state level is that if you compare liberal/socialist states like California, New York and Massachusetts with "conservative" states like Texas and Utah you will see that the small government model ALWAYS results in greater freedom and wealth for the people at all levels.

So what are the states prohibited from doing? Article 1 Section 10 lists the few things states can't do. States can not enter into any treaty, alliance or confederation with another country, grant letters of marquee and reprisal, coin money, emit bills of credit, pass bills of attainder, ex post facto laws, impair contractual obligations, grant titles of nobility, lay any import, export or tonnage duties without the consent and control of Congress or maintain a military without Congress' consent.

As you can see most of the powers prohibited to the states deals with international law and commerce so, as abhorrent as it is, socialism is authorized at the state level. The reason we so often see left imposing socialism at the national vice state level is that were a state to enact socialized medicine, for example, it would perform so poorly compared to a free market state as to completely disprove Marxist theories.

THE PRESIDENCY

The powers and responsibilities delegated to the president are even narrower than those of the legislature. Article 2 Section 2 of the Constitution designates the President as Commander-in-Chief of the armed forces, permits him to grant pardons and reprieves, negotiate treaties and appoint public officials. Clearly the Founding Fathers did not intend for the Presidency to be the preeminent force in government. However, they did intend for him to be the most active.

How can that be? It seems incongruent with our modern sensibilities that the executive could be the most active branch of government and at the same time *not* be the most powerful. The intent was for the legislature to control the agenda with regard to public policy and for the president to have jurisdiction in cases that required quick action. As Alexander Hamilton explained in Federalist #70, the executive should be the most active branch in government, but only in executing the laws established by Congress and repelling foreign invasion.

Energy in the Executive is a leading character in the definition of good government. It is essential to the protection of the community against foreign attacks; it is not less essential to the steady administration of the laws; to the protection of property against those irregular and high-handed combinations, which sometimes interrupt the ordinary course of justice; to the security of liberty against the enterprises and assaults of ambition, of faction, and of anarchy...

A feeble Executive implies a feeble execution of the government. A feeble execution is but another phrase for a bad execution; and a government ill executed, whatever it may be in theory, must be, in practice, a bad government.[96]

Today we have turned this idea on its head. Presidents spend most of their effort concocting public policy initiatives (which the Congress either blindly supports or vilifies based on its majority party affiliation) all the while refusing to perform their constitutional duty in securing the borders from illegal immigration which is no less a violation of our national sovereignty than an invasion from a foreign army.

---

[96] Hamilton, Alexander. Federalist #70: *The Executive Department Further Considered.* March 18th 1788

Chapter 9
The Right Way Forward

There can be no doubt that Americans have built the greatest nation in the history of mankind. Never before or since has a country been built entirely on the ideals of liberty, God given individual rights and limited government. Imagine what the world would be like without America. There would be no Bill of Rights. Chances are the philosophies of John Locke and Adam Smith would have been completely extinguished in favor of tyrannical doctrines.

Mankind may not have ever enjoyed so many of the inventions that have changed our lives. There are, of course, the obvious. The light bulb, computer, telephone and airplane were created by Americans, but less obvious and in many ways just as important are the can opener, blue jeans, gas masks, blood banks, the telegraph and the phonograph.

Countless other inventions only reached their full potential because of Americans' ingenuity and the free market that inspired them. An American may not have invented the automobile, but where would that invention or the state of our freedom of movement be without Henry Ford's assembly line? Rockets existed since ancient China, but it was America that used them to put men on the moon and now the entire world enjoys all the derivative technologies.

How is it that in less than 235 years America has accomplished more and benefited mankind more than other countries that have existed for thousands of years? It can't be said that we are a superior race, because America is comprised of every race. No, the reason Americans have been able to accomplish so much is that for most of our history our forefathers enjoyed a freedom from government intrusion never before imagined. Edison invented the light bulb and the Wright Brothers invented the airplane without government grants. The pioneers crossed the prairies and tamed the Rockies without a dime of stimulus money.

Sadly, America is no longer the great nation that did all those things. Once Americans took up arms and sacrificed everything to fight a British government that was at the time the freest, most classically liberal government in the world because they recognized it infringed on their rights. They braved cannon and cold, death and starvation to secure a government that would do as little as possible to them... and for them.

Today we live in a country where the government, in some cases, takes more than half of what an individual earns and divides it among people who do nothing. We live in a country where many expect the government to do everything for them at the expense of the hard working entrepreneur and the population that would otherwise benefit from their efforts. Worst of all we live in a country where few truly understand the nature of their rights or responsibilities as citizens. America, like Rome and Athens before, is collapsing under its own largesse. We are slowly dooming our children to a country where the government and not the people are sovereign.

Fortunately there is hope. I believe America is a nation with a destiny. A destiny yet unfulfilled to bring freedom to all mankind by being a beacon of liberty for all to emulate. The following is a list of things we must do to get back on the right track as a nation. They are not easy solutions. In fact some are quite radical, but the moment we commit ourselves to the right course we will see improvements in our society. With commitment, hard work and sacrifice Americans can do anything.

The Economy

The best solution our government can give for our economic woes is to get out of the way! We must eliminate corporate and personal income taxes altogether. These taxes punish success and worst of all presume that the money we earn somehow belongs first to the government. Eliminating them would not only free up trillions of dollars for the economy, but would create a more just society. The only moral forms of taxation are consumption and property taxes, because they allow people to choose how much they pay in taxes. If someone decides to spend their wealth on flashy cars and electronics instead of investing it in the economy then they will pay more in taxes than someone who chooses to save and live frugally. Shouldn't we use our tax policy to encourage rather than discourage frugality?

A national sales tax would be more than sufficient to cover our national needs if we confine government spending to *only* those actions specifically enumerated in the Constitution.

Government Spending

So much of what is wrong with America comes from our zeal to overspend in the pursuit of helping the so called 'downtrodden'. Besides being unconstitutional, the redistribution of wealth does not work. It only creates more poverty. We must gradually eliminate all spending on social welfare. Nowhere in the Constitution is the Federal Government authorized to redistribute wealth. Federal spending must be confined to constitutionally mandated spending like supporting the military, operating the post office and maintaining roads used for interstate commerce. This would so dramatically reduce government spending that only a nominal federal sales tax would be required to support national level policies.

National Security

In some ways national security reform is the most difficult issue, because it involves fundamentally changing America's last sacred cow; the military. However, national security goes far beyond having a strong military.

First and foremost we must begin tapping all of our natural resources. This will allow us to divest ourselves from some of the concerns of the Middle East and save us trillions in treasure and countless lives in the long run. Yes it may take several years to get some of these sites up and running, but we must take a long-term view towards national security. Our competitors: India, China and the Islamic world generally have a worldview that spans centuries while we can't see past the next Congressional budget.

Second, we must restructure our military. Our large standing military is ideal for fending off Soviet hordes, but is it the right fit for a republic in an age where large-scale invasion is once again no longer a threat? I think we would benefit greatly from a complete reevaluation of our national security structure with the aim of brining it more in line with the Founder's view mentioned in Chapter 7. Sure the military-industrial complex may lose billions of dollars, but our government's most important job is to protect our rights, not the bottom line of fortune 500 companies.

The Judiciary

We must add a check and balance to our legal system, by allowing legislatures of equal rank to overturn judicial decisions. For example, if the US Supreme Court renders an opinion contrary to the public will the US Congress could overturn the decision. This would be the most fundamentally radical change to US jurisprudence since the signing of the Constitution. However, I think legislatures would be so reluctant to overturn all but the most egregious miscarriages of justice that only a simple majority should be required.

In the end, though, there is only one solution to the problem of our overreaching judiciary. It is actually the same solution to every problem we have, an active and vigilant populace. As voters we must reject all politicians who do not explicitly support strict constructionist judges and reject the deeply flawed legal philosophies of people like Ruth Bader Ginsberg. When judges, even those appointed for lifetime terms, violate this most sacred trust with the people they must be subject to impeachment.

The Entitlement Culture

Far and away the largest threat to the future of America is the entitlement culture. By entitlement culture I mean that segment of society that believes government should redistribute the wealth of certain citizens for the personal gain of others. And that segment is larger than you might think. It is not just lazy individuals who would rather live their entire lives on welfare than work an honest job. Those individuals make up a very small portion of our society. The entitlement culture also includes people who believe things like health care, housing and retirement are rights that the government must provide for the people.

This is a very slippery slope we are on. It is a slippery slope that ends with government confiscating the majority of everyone's wealth to feed an increasingly inefficient and corrupt bureaucracy. Meanwhile the people become so dependent on government largesse that they forget how to provide even the most basic necessities for themselves.

Remember in chapter one when we learned how this entitlement culture and its attendant socialism brought Rome to its knees? The most powerful empire in the world slowly rotted away from within, because the people demanded the government do everything for them. Their civic virtue and work ethic deteriorated to the point where they refused to defend their eternal city or even bake their own bread without government handouts.

We are repeating the same mistakes and the results are all around us. Europe is plagued by riots when politicians even suggest cutting government spending. We print or borrow trillions of dollars to continue our socialist programs. This is nothing more than generational theft. Our children and grandchildren will have to pay the bills for our reckless spending. To make matters worse our economy is slowly sliding into irrelevance on the world stage as the government consumes a rapidly increasing portion of the GDP, thus condemning our children to pay our bills with smaller paychecks than we make now.

So how do we reverse this trend and regain the prosperity and freedom that make this country so great? Not surprisingly the answer can't be found in government. Sure we must vote only for politicians who promise to cut spending and taxes, but inevitably politicians will disappoint us if we rely too much on them. Indeed, the answer lies within each of us. We must become more active citizens. There are literally millions of ways for each of us to contribute to the betterment of society. Join the school board so you can ensure your children are learning the right things in school. Run for city council or become more active in religious and charitable organizations. Above all, get your own house in order and secure for yourself a future of financial independence so you will not be seduced by the opiate that is government entitlement spending. After all fiscal responsibility begins at home, not Washington.

If we simply muster the courage to take charge of our own lives and be the independent, rugged individuals our ancestors were we could do anything. But first we must relearn the wisdom of our Founding Fathers and hold our government accountable when it acts outside the boundaries of the Constitution. John Adams once said "Remember, democracy never lasts long. It soon wastes, exhausts, and murders itself. There is never a democracy that did not commit suicide."[97] Let's prove him wrong.

---

[97] John Adams, letter to John Taylor, April 15, 1814

Afterword

Writing this book has been an incredibly enlightening experience. Like most college educated Americans, I've always thought I had a good grasp on the history and philosophy of our nation's founding. Additionally I have been an avid reader of colonial era history my entire adult life, but in researching for this book I learned so much more than I imagined and have often been surprised by the misconceptions I possessed before undertaking this journey. For example, I always thought the Founders had fairly uniform views on the role of religion in society. I was shocked by just how different the opinions of Washington, and Adams were from Jefferson and Madison. And I was inspired by how these men could arrange their differing opinions in a way that best suited the country. Another point of enlightenment that humbled me was in trying to find the one principle that could be said to be the philosophical foundation of America. I have long thought it was Locke's principles of property rights. Indeed I still do, but through researching and reading the Declaration of Independence and Constitution I was almost convinced that I should elevate the doctrine of popular sovereignty, especially over the judiciary, to the founding principle. Eventually I came to the conclusion that even that is secondary to the maintenance of our property rights.

It is my sincere hope that after reading this book you have become a more informed and responsible citizen of our great republic. I would like to leave you what I believe is one of the most moving quotes of any Founding Father. It is attributed to Dr. Joseph Warren shortly before he was killed leading the charge for freedom at Bunker Hill in 1775 and repeated by President Ronald Reagan when he took the Oath of Office.

Our country is in danger, but not to be despaired of... On you depend the fortunes of America. You are to decide the important questions upon which rests the happiness and liberty of millions yet unborn. Act worthy of yourselves.[98]

---

[98] Bennett, William J. America: The Last Best Hope.p481 Nashville, TN. 2007

www.ingramcontent.com/pod-product-compliance
Lightning Source LLC
Chambersburg PA
CBHW072211280526
45788CB00002B/967